Native American Fiction
A User's Manual

Native American Fiction

A USER'S MANUAL

David Treuer

Graywolf Press
SAINT PAUL, MINNESOTA

Publication of this volume is made possible in part by a grant
provided by the Minnesota State Arts Board, through an ap-
propriation by the Minnesota State Legislature; a grant from
the Wells Fargo Foundation Minnesota; and a grant from
the National Endowment for the Arts, which believes that a
great nation deserves great art. Significant support has also
been provided by the Bush Foundation; Target; the McKnight
Foundation; and other generous contributions from foundations, corporations, and individuals. To these organizations and
individuals we offer our heartfelt thanks.

MINNESOTA
STATE ARTS BOARD

NATIONAL
ENDOWMENT
FOR THE ARTS

Published by Graywolf Press
2402 University Avenue, Suite 203
Saint Paul, Minnesota 55114
All rights reserved.

www.graywolfpress.org

Published in the United States of America

ISBN-10: 1-55597-452-X
ISBN-13: 978-1-55597-452-7

2 4 6 8 9 7 5 3 1
First Graywolf Printing, 2006

Library of Congress Control Number: 2006924340

Cover design: Kyle G. Hunter
Cover photograph: ©Veer

for my brother
Anton Steven Treuer

~

whose efforts to save and promote
the Ojibwe language
are unequalled and are the most precious gift
to us all

Contents

Native American Fiction
A User's Manual

Author's Note

To study literature is to study the manifestation and manipulation of the written word and the weight of tradition behind those words. So-called Native American fiction (if there is such a thing) has not been studied, *as literature,* as much as it should be. By applying ourselves to the word, and, at least at the outset of our endeavors, by ignoring the identity of the author and all the ways the author constructs his or her authority outside the text, we will be better able to ascertain the true value of that text. It seems strange that we greet the claims of drug companies and politicians with caution and care, never believing what they say about their products, yet we often rest our judgment on the expressed sentiments of this or that author. A Native American novel is not a Native American novel simply or only because an Indian wrote it, or because someone who is Indian claims that the product of his/her imagination (always a messy thing) is fundamentally and essentially Indian. Over the last thirty years Native American fiction has been defined as, exclusively, literature written by Indians. And this collection of essays might be seen as a dangerous turning back of the clock, or the rapid undoing of three decades of hard work by critics and authors. However, the sentiment (and it *is* a sentiment) that Native American literature should be defined by the ethnicity of its producers (more so than defined by anything else) says more about politics and identity than it does about literature. This is especially true, and especially clear, when we see that our books are constructed out of the same materials available to anyone else. Ultimately, the study of Native American fiction should be the study of style. Native Americans, more so than any other group, are experienced through image and text and story more so than through shared, lived experience. How we are created and recreated on the page, by ourselves and others, is the matter at hand. Indian authors as well as critics are no less permeable, no less susceptible to received images and ideas that come together to create the convincing narratives found in novels.

I am concerned with how we *read* so-called Native American texts, how to interpret Native American fiction in such a way as to take pleasure in the product, and how to interpret it so as to preserve the integrity of the text, the integrity of our own interest and effort, and the integrity of the tradition.

This book is not concerned with questions of authenticity—what is or what is not an authentic Indian text. The terrible twins—identity and authenticity—do need proper rearing, and there might be a time and place when it is necessary to treat them, but this is not that time or place. This book does not seek to define what is or what should be seen as Native American literature and is not involved with the new essentialist project of defining only texts in Native American languages as authentic Indian texts and those in English merely fantasies in the conqueror's language. Rather, this is a book about interpretation: about what is gained and what is lost when we interpret Native American fiction with more stress placed on "Native" than on "fiction." As such, this collection of essays is concerned with how novels act, not with how authors or critics would like them to or what we think the author's intention was: I am concerned with echo not origin.

It is crucial to make a distinction between reading books *as* culture and seeing books as capable of *suggesting* culture. It is equally as important to leave aside questions of authenticity and identity (if only for the moment) in order to re-center our interpretive efforts: to un-wed ourselves from looking at Indian fiction in terms of origination and to start thinking of it in terms of destination; that is, interpretation not production. If we can force ourselves to read Native American fiction we will find style, not culture. Or, rather, we will find that, as far as literature is concerned, style IS culture; style creates the convincing semblance of culture on the page. Then the real question becomes: what traditions and habits of thought have been mobilized and by what means in Native American fiction?

Many of the good books dealt with here get what could be seen as fairly harsh treatment. The novels treated in this book, with two exceptions, are all great novels, and this collection of essays takes issue more with how these books are interpreted (by their authors, critics, and their readers) than with how they are constructed. I believe that by not taking the literature seriously, by handing out praise where it is not earned, by obscuring the workings of a novel with claims for culture or tradition not supported by the text, we run a great and terrible risk. It is important to remember that we are entering textual fantasies here, not a sweat lodge. That is, despite what the books might mean to us, as individuals or as Indians, the books function as books. By making sweeping claims about the culturality of a text or the intentionality of the writer we might save the book, but we will destroy the literature. I side with T. S. Eliot in thinking that a great literature only survives when it is lofted on the shoulders of great readers.

The Clouds Overhead

We are used to thinking of fiction and scholarship as two distinct, autonomous kinds of knowledge: related, but ultimately, revolving around separate suns. While it is tempting to see fiction as creating different, new, sometimes explosive amounts of meaning, and scholarship as content to undo the beautiful, complicated damage of art, this stance is ultimately unsatisfactory. For me, both writing and criticism should try—by recombining the elements of meaning (sometimes under the guise of reality, at other times masquerading as fantasy) that continually float around us—to create something as new and exciting as our materials are. R. P. Blackmur went so far as to suggest:

> Like walking, criticism is a pretty nearly
> universal art; both require a constant intri-
> cate shifting and catching of balance; neither
> can be questioned much in process; and few
> perform either really well.[1]

At the present moment, I am concerned with reading as an inherently critical activity. To understand it as such we need to untell a lie we've been told about reading. To read and engage with a story is not to "suspend disbelief." That is a lie. Rather, to read and engage and love and consume and consummate a relationship with a story is to believe. And belief is a critical, if sometimes unconscious, habit we practice. How we practice it, what we are accustomed to believing in literature, and what we cannot accept are matters of training.

But before I was either a writer or a scholar, I was a reader. Where I grew up there wasn't much around except books and trees. So I developed the habit of climbing the trees behind our house, and swaying in the wind, reading the day away. Late in the afternoon I would hear the door slam and my mother's voice calling me down to dinner. When I heard her, faintly, from below, I quit reading and climbed down as fast as I could and ran for the house. I knew that if I didn't hurry, my older brother would eat all the mashed potatoes before I got there. "Food's history, man," he'd say as he lathered his potatoes with butter, and I stared forlornly at the empty serving bowl. He grew up to be a historian. While, as Blackmur would have it, criticism is as common as walking, I suspect I might actually be running. Perhaps old habits die hard, maybe I am still running, as quickly as my legs allow, toward those disappearing potatoes. My only hope is that I won't, like I so often did, leave my books behind, splayed over a branch in the top of a tree. I can see the pages greeting the bark as descendants meet their ancestors, only without me to make the introduction.

Wonder

In March of 1860, Charles Baudelaire went to see and hear Wagner's opera *Tannhauser* during its Paris debut. His lyric music had the most profound effect on the French poet. It filled him with a mysterious, acute, voluptuous sensation. Baudelaire spent the next thirteen months obsessed with both Wagner's magic and its effect. As he states in his essay on Wagner, published in 1861, "I determined to discover the why and wherefore, and thus transform my sensuous pleasure to knowledge."[2]

Three years to the day after Baudelaire published his famous essay, across the Atlantic wonder was making a different kind of appearance. On April 9, 1863, a delegation of Western chiefs traveled to Washington, D.C., to meet with President Lincoln. They had come east at the behest of the American government that, caught in the midst of the Civil War, was afraid of another uprising like the Dakota conflict that consumed Minnesota in 1862. The Western tribes were still very powerful and it was thought that their influence on their own people could turn the tide of the Civil War. After their meeting with Lincoln they were induced to travel to New York where they "performed" at Barnum's American Museum. Among the chiefs present were War Bonnet, Lean Bear, and Hand-in-the-Water of the Cheyenne; Yellow Buffalo and Yellow Bear of the Kiowas; Jacob of the Caddos; and White Bull of the Apaches. Their performances at Barnum's American Museum consisted of the chiefs standing silently on the stage in full regalia while Barnum spun yarns about their bloodthirsty ferocity. Trips were arranged to area schools. They met the mayor. But it seems the chiefs weren't aware they were on display: Barnum had arranged it secretly with their interpreter. In his memoirs Barnum wrote that once the chiefs found out they had been conned, he feared for his life and was only too happy to see them go. But Barnum's life wasn't the one in danger: within eighteen months after their departure, chiefs Yellow Buffalo, Yellow Bear, and Standing-in-the-Water were shot down at the Sand Creek massacre.

Around the same time, near Ash River, Lean Bear's band of Cheyenne came upon a contingent of U.S. Cavalry. Lean Bear went out with another warrior to meet with them wearing the Presidential Medal given to him by President Lincoln. When he was twenty or thirty yards away, the soldiers all opened fire on Lean Bear. The soldiers then rode forward and shot Lean Bear again as he lay helpless on the ground.[3]

For Baudelaire, Wagner was something to be wondered *about,* whereas the chiefs were a phenomenon to be wondered *at.* Why did Wagner make Baudelaire want to transform his wonder into knowledge, whereas the chiefs—sublime, otherworldly, important, and precious—were reduced to a curiosity? The cheap answer is that Barnum was more interested in transforming wonder into money, but it is more

NATIVE AMERICAN FICTION: A USER'S MANUAL

than that. How, in life and literature, can Indians remain so knowable and so strange at the same time? How can we be so distant and so immediately accessible—especially to and in the imagination, whereas in life we are, to most, impenetrable? One need only remember Thompson's ubiquitous series of piano method books, where in volume one we learn, in C Major, to play and sing—*I know what the Indian knows, I go where the Indian goes.* Curiously, Native American fiction is also on silent display, with readers and critics willing to wonder at, but rarely about, its presence. And it seems to me that what motivates Indian fiction remains largely unsaid, and it works precisely because of these timely silences.

Silence

Indian silence is a strange thing. Indians make up 1 percent of the population of the United States—two million out of two hundred million. Yet we Indians overpopulate the modern imagination—from the first Thanksgiving to the Boston Tea Party to Longfellow's *Song of Hiawatha* to the Battle of the Little Big Horn to *Dances with Wolves.* The Indians people imagine, and the Indians that are created on the page, are much more active, much more present, than the Indians in life. The result is a very loud silence. Ours is a ghostly presence. The problem is that ghosts don't express themselves well—they throw things and move furniture, they speak through mediums, and despite the awe that their visitations instill, they can be manipulated and misinterpreted.

Nowhere is our silent presence more apparent than in the writing of William Gilmore Simms. Most likely, the name of William Gilmore Simms will not be familiar to most readers. In his long career Simms published dozens of romances, stories, and novels, four volumes of verse, three histories, a book of Shakespeare apocrypha, and scores of essays and critiques.[4] *The Yemassee,* published in 1835, was to be his most widely read and critically acclaimed novel. Set on the Carolina coast in 1715, *The Yemassee* weaves together history, action, and intrigue during the Indian uprising in that year against the British colonists.

Unlike James Fenimore Cooper's much more well-known and widely read *Leatherstocking Tales,* which uses Indian wars as a battleground for the all-important question of what kind of identity America would have, Simms was actually interested in the clash of two vastly different cultures. While both authors, perhaps, were looking for a mirror in which to see the face of America, Cooper was more concerned with the reflection and Simms with the makeup of the glass.

The Yemassee is hardly a "good" novel, but it is a fascinating one. With the fate of the colony hovering over every page of the novel, we learn of two cultures in conflict. The Natives—represented by Sanutee, the Chief, his wife Matiwan, and their son Occonestoga—are faced with the tough decision of whether they should rise up against the British or not, while the colonists are torn as to whether they should trust the tribes with whom they have been peacefully (from the colonists' perspective) allied, or if they need to gear up in preparation for future hostilities. Thrown into the mix is a budding love connection between Bess Matthews and the mysterious Captain Harrison (whose real identity as Charles Craven, the governor of the Carolinas, is, as Hugh Holman suggests, the worst-kept secret in American fiction).[5] If this weren't complicated enough, Simms, to his discredit and any reader's numbing dismay, felt that what was lacking in historical romances (such as *Ivanhoe*) was metaphysical insight; and the characters, particularly Hugh Grayson and Matiwan, have protracted, agonizing moments of self-doubt that go on for pages.

It is hard to be kind to *The Yemassee*. Even in its day it was filled with what amount to stereotyped characters: devious Indians, fainting maidens, not-so-secret identities. He created rough and ready frontiersmen with names like Wat Grayson and Dick Mason. The Indian chief Sanutee speaks to his wife in the third person (as if Indians are so out of place and out of time—doomed to live lives of death—that we can't even know ourselves well enough to use the first person), while (over by the fort) Harrison calls Bess Matthews "my sweet, my rosebud" and more such Valentine rubbish. The action speeds and stills around timely arrivals, hairbreadth escapes, and metaphysical wondering, but still manages to rumble to the final confrontation at the settlers' crude fort.

Miraculously, despite the book's drawbacks (and its reliance on stereotype), Simms was able to create psychologically complex Indian and white characters, none of whom are either all good or all bad.

As the introduction to the 1961 edition suggests, in Cooper it is necessary to add Uncas to Magua to get a fully realized character, whereas in *The Yemassee,* such magic is not necessary.[6] Simms is at pains to show Indian daily life, Indian lifeways, if only to better understand what is really going on here—Indian death.

"You will note," wrote Simms in the preface to the 1853 edition, "that I call 'The Yemassee' a Romance, and not a novel. You will permit me to insist upon the distinction."[7] The distinction was clear and had been for quite some time before 1853, but he continued.

> The question briefly is—What are the standards of the modern Romance? What is the modern Romance itself? . . . . The modern Romance is the substitute which the people of the present day offer for the ancient epic. The form is changed: the matter is very much the same: at all events, it differs much more seriously from the English novel. . . . The domestic novel is confined to the felicitous narration of common and daily occurring events, and the grouping and delineation of characters in ordinary conditions of society.[8]

Ironically, just as the Pyncheon family can hear, or imagine they do, the faint stirrings of Maule's ghost in *The House of the Seven Gables,* we have to imagine *we* hear an echo of Nathaniel Hawthorne's introduction to that novel (written in 1851) in Simms's 1853 preface. Hawthorne asserted:

When a writer calls his work a Romance, it
need hardly be observed that he wishes to
claim a certain latitude, both as to its fashion
and material, which he would not have felt
himself entitled to assume, had he professed
to be writing a Novel. . . . The point of view
in which this Tale comes under the Romantic
definition, lies in the attempt to connect a by-
gone time with the very Present that is flitting
away from us.[9]

For Simms, though, a Romance was defined by
more than its handling of historical material. For him
an American Romance necessarily involved Native
Americans. *"The Yemassee,"* he stated, "is proposed
as an American Romance. It is so styled as much of
the material could have been furnished by no other
country."[10]

While no other country could furnish the material necessary for an American Romance, there
was, for Simms, a connection between the genocide of Native Americans and Western literary texts
that made his material what it was. It is no coinci-
dence that Simms saw three stage productions in
Charleston in 1831 before going out to the Indian ter-
ritories to visit his father. He happened to see John
August Stone's *Metamora* (a play about King Phil-
lip's uprising against the colonists in 1675), Sheridan
Knowles's *Virginius; or, the Roman Father,* and John
Howard Payne's *Brutus; or, The Fall of Tarquin* within
a span of three weeks. As Hugh Holman's brilliant introduction to the 1961 edition of *The Yemassee* notes,

it is no wonder that when he wrote of Chief William McIntosh a few short months after seeing these plays he said that the chief's death "had something of the Roman in it."[11]

In literature (and in life) Indians don't simply die: like the Romans in dramatic literature their corporeal selves are, from the moment they are born, catching up with their fated selves. It is not a question of whether Indians or Roman heroes will live, but when and how they will die. No one, to reach further back, really thinks Oedipus will ever be happy. And like Oedipus, what happens to Indians is the blossoming of hidden knowledge of the bloody past. Or, if not fated, Indian death is never private, it is always attended by larger meanings—and unlike the Pyncheons of the *Seven Gables,* Indians don't have the luxury of being haunted by someone else, they haunt themselves. And if they aren't dead by the end of the book, it's only a matter of time.

Death isn't the only thing, however hidden, that informs Native American literary presences, but it is a cardinal one. They were also vested with nobility, strength, even savage sensibilities, and, to be fair, no small amount of humanity. But it is death that gives fictional Indians their power. Death grants them a knowing essence. And Indians in fiction—from the books of Simms and Cooper up to Erdrich and Alexie—function as knowing ghosts whose presence alone speaks back in time to the crimes committed against them.

Seen this way, there was no need for Barnum or

NATIVE AMERICAN FICTION: A USER'S MANUAL

his audience to explore the "why and wherefore" of the chiefs on exhibit in his American museum. Even though they, for the most part, remained silent, their presence spoke volumes. They literally *went without saying.* The existence of the chiefs in New York City made of them a paradox of meaning—their presence was at once strange and, it was thought, immediately knowable.

Surplus

Linked to the idea of silence is the idea of surplus. The best example of this is the history of the "Chant to the Fire-fly."

The chant was first recorded by the explorer and ethnologist Henry Rowe Schoolcraft in the early nineteenth century and published by him in 1845 in *Oneota, or the Red Race of America.* It reads as follows:

> Wau wau tay see!
> Wau wau tay see!
> E mow e shin
> Tshe bwau ne baun-e wee!
> Be eghaun—be eghaun—e wee!
> Wa wau tay see!
> Wa wau tay see!
> Was sa koon ain je gun
> Was sa koon ain je gun.[12]

Schoolcraft then offered two translations, one "literal" and one "literary":

Flitting-white-fire-insect! Waving-white-fire-bug! Give me light before I go to bed! Give me light before I go to sleep. Come, little dancing white-fire-bug! Come, little flitting white-fire-insect! Light me with your bright white-flame instrument—your little candle.

The "literary" translation eschews the prose form in favor of verse:

Fire-fly, fire-fly! bright little thing,
Light me to bed, and my song I will sing.
Give me your light, as you fly o'er my head,
That I may merrily go to my bed.[13]

And that was just the beginning. After Schoolcraft, Henry Wadsworth Longfellow, who relied heavily on Schoolcraft's ethnography for his American epic, *The Song of Hiawatha*, inserted the chant into the third part of his poem. The chant was included in every reprinting of both Schoolcraft's work and Longfellow's poem. It has been retranslated, reinterpreted, and reworked. The chant was discussed in scholarly work beginning in the late nineteenth century, and periodically during the twentieth century. The little chant has become famous, a kind of textual Shirley Temple—innocent and poetic at the same time. Not high art, but art nonetheless, and whatever its merits, it was, as John Nichols, points out, "the most well-known Native American poem" in the nineteenth century.[14]

In the original Ojibwe text that Schoolcraft recorded there are only five different words. (here I use the double-vowel orthography preferred by modern linguists): *waawaatesi, waawaatese'amawishin, jibwaa-nibaayaan, bi-izhaan, waasakonenjigan.*

1. *Waawaatesi.* This word means "fire-fly."
   [If we look at the morphemes separately we see the morpheme for light *-waa* is re-duplicated and so suggests a wavering or aimless, or intermittent, quality. And we have *-te*—the middle reflexive inanimate verb final "-te" suggests "by heat." And *-si* (or *-siw* in abstract form), which is a noun ending often used to designate insects or other small creatures.]

2. *Waawaatese'amawishin.* This is a verb (sort of), and it is harder to translate. [We have the word for fire-fly, changed slightly at the end (*-tese* as opposed to *-tesi*). The change has two effects, one literal and the other poetic. The *-tese* ending suggests "fly, skip, happen spontaneously" and so, in a literal sense, *waawaatese* means flickering light, and in some dialects is the word for aurora borealis. In the poetic sense, the whole word *waawaatese,* in the context of the chant, brings the concept of the fire-fly with it, even though, after the slight change, the word has nothing, literally, to do with fire-flies. Fixed to that we have the glottal stop *-'-,* which makes the verb transitive as opposed to the intransitive "make someone do something," and, *-amaw-,*

which is a benefactive final that means "do for somebody." Finally -*ishin*, which inflects the verb—a second- to first-person command. Imagine a trucker in a diner telling the waitress to "coffee me" when he wants a refill and you will have the English equivalent, or the closest we can get.]

3. *Jibwaa*. Before.
4. *Nibaayaan*. As or when I sleep.
5. *Bi-izhaan*. Come here.
6. *Waasakonenjigan*. Lantern or candle.

The words in the chant are simple, the verb forms simple, and the structure simpler still. All this beautiful little piece ever was or was ever meant to be is a children's nursery rhyme (though Ojibwe children didn't really have nurseries). The only reason it has survived is through chance and luck.

By going back to Schoolcraft's two translations, and moving forward, we can see how, almost immediately, surplus meanings and surplus words have crept in and supplanted the original meanings. By my count, Schoolcraft uses at least eight extra words, whose meaning does not appear in the original Ojibwe, in his literal translation. He graciously gives the chant *flitting, white, fire, bed, little, dancing, beast, bright,* and *instrument*. His literary translation, half as long, manages to include just as many: *bright, little, song, sing, fly, over, head, merrily,* and *bed*.

The critic and translator, Dell Hymes, who does not know the Ojibwe language, has suggested that it is fortunate we have the original text if only because "thanks to Schoolcraft's scholarship, we can appreciate in depth how bad his translation is."[15] One wonders how Hymes arrived at his own "translation," and how he is able to tell whether or not a given translation is "bad" or "good" without being able to understand the original. Hymes offers his own translation:

Flitting insect of white fire!
Flitting insect of white fire!
Come, give me light before I sleep!
Come, give me light before I sleep!
Flitting insect of white fire!
Flitting insect of white fire!
Light me with your bright instrument of flame.
Light me with your bright instrument of flame.[16]

Hymes manages to pare it down, but the sense he derives from the chant does not seem to come from the chant itself. He only includes *white* and *fire* and *bright*. What is interesting is that even though Hymes excoriates Schoolcraft for bad translation, these words (white, fire, bright) come from Schoolcraft's English, not from the Ojibwe. Hymes relies more on Schoolcraft than he does on the Ojibwe original. Moreover, the structure of Hymes's translation with the duplication of each line, ostensibly meant to suggest the kind of repetition one sees in some Native American songs, is drastically misapplied here. And in a bizarre twist, it may have more to do with the apparent simplicity of, say, the poetry of Robert Frost, than with any kind of Native American, much less Ojibwe, performance.

> And miles to go before I sleep,
> And miles to go before I sleep.

Interpretation is always a risky business. The interpretation of Indian literature is particularly risky. The "Chant to the Fire-fly" is only one instance of wild and willful misinterpretation, and a minor one at that. But by looking at the poor fire-fly we can see clearly how meaning upon meaning is grafted onto the initial slender stalk; how the original sense bends under the weight. I think it is somewhat perverse that so much can be said about a thing without understanding the thing. The same kind of perversion is visited on Indian novels on a much grander scale. The chant is vulnerable because those commenting on it rarely know the original language. Novels are vulnerable for a different reason because they can, through their own multiplicity, suggest whatever we want them to. Indian novels are even more vulnerable because of the compounding silence I mentioned earlier and the ubiquitous presence Indians have in the American literary and mythic landscape. As for "The Chant to the Fire-fly," though it has suffered much, it can still winkle as it's meant to. So much has been made of so little that the chant's own unique and beautiful sense has been dwarfed by its interpretation. A translation more in keeping with the words and the moment and the light quality of children's rhyme, might be:

Firefly, fire fly and flit for me
Fly for me before I sleep
Firefly fire fly
Lantern! Lantern!

Surplus is something intrepid interpreters have to watch out for. It is relatively easy to pare off the rind of interpretation that encrusts this chant. It is more difficult to do that for Indian novels. Whenever critics make claims for the "trickster motif" in Sherman Alexie's writing, or of "tribal" ways of storytelling, or make some other heavy but seemingly limpid claim for Indian fiction, I always think of how when I was a child we used to collect fire-flies in peanut butter jars and keep them by our beds at night, shaking them every once in a while to make them glow brighter. They are delicate things, though. And, trapped behind the glass, rigorously shaken, they were always dead by morning.

Perhaps it's all backwards, and when Alexander Pope declaimed "Lo, The poor Indian!" he really meant "Lo, the poor Native American literary critic!":

Whose untutor'd mind
Sees God in clouds, or hears Him in the wind;
His soul, proud Science never taught to stray
Far as the solar-walk, or milky-way;
Yet simple Nature to his hope has given,
Behind the cloud-topp'd hill, and humbler Heaven,
Some safer world in depth of woods embraced,
Some happier island in the watery waste,[17]

Indian Tears

Reading Indians as exemplars (of culture, of disappearance, of recovery) or as civilization's ghosts has been carried forward into what we consider modern Native American fiction. This is, in a large part, what makes Indian fiction work. On the first day of my Native American Fiction class this winter, I read a line from Sherman Alexie's story "Every Little Hurricane":

"Victor watched his father cry huge, gasping tears. Indian Tears."[18]

I asked my students to write down what those Indian tears signified. To my amazement, as if unearthing whole mastodons from the soil of their imaginative backyards, without ever having read any Native American fiction, my students asserted that, and I quote, "Indian tears represent the loss of land, culture and language. They show what it feels like to be dispossessed of everything." And, my favorite: "Indian tears are for pain and suffering at the hands of the white man—just like the tears are of the African American man in the ghetto." Alexie deftly intuited (I am not sure we can say he intended) his readers' automatic response to the phrase and image of "Indian tears" thereby mobilizing what the reader thinks he knows about Indians.

Unfortunately for Alexie and for us, when a story is built on supposition and received ideas it can't ever rise above those suppositions. The house of text will have the same footprint as the automatic thought. The result is the kind of sentiment that Alexie most abhors—a form of knowingness based on nothing.

"Indian tears" has led my students, upon finishing the story, to say they now knew what it was like to be Indian, how it was to feel Indian. (I can hear the strain's of Thompson's pentatonic chant "I know what the Indian knows" bleeding through again.) Alexie's "Indian tears" should remind us that most readers come to Native literature fully loaded with ideas, images, and notions, and that the process of interpretation needs to take this into account. How does one escape this all-pervading thing, exoticized foreknowledge?

Hawthorne believed that *The House of the Seven Gables* should be seen as a legend, "prolonging itself, from an epoch now gray in the distance, down into our own broad daylight, and bringing along with it some of its legendary mist. . . . having a great deal more to do with the clouds overhead, than with any portion of the actual soil of the County of Essex."[19] That is precisely what Alexie's "Indian tears" and our concepts of Indian culture do—they bring with them the legendary mist of Indian misery. And, like *The House of the Seven Gables*, Native American fiction has more to do with the clouds overhead than with any portion of American earth, whether it be Pueblo sand or Essex soil. None of this is to say that modern Native American literature hasn't managed to create mists and magic of its own. Nor that its destiny is in any way more enslaved to the literary past than the destinies of other genres—to suggest otherwise would be to make the position of Native American literature as tragic and static and painfully unavoidable as the fate of the Yemassee Indians in Simms's book.

My argument is not about how Native American fiction is created. I am concerned with how it is read; how we, like Blackmur, walk toward it. To interpret and criticize Native American fiction successfully I suspect we need both our moccasins and our hobnails, our buckskin vests and our leather jerkins. To see Native American literature as linked with American literature; to see culture as an active character in modern novels (much in the same way as haunted houses are in Romances) instead of reading novels *as culture,* that is, as products of difference rather than as attempts to create it; to see things this way makes our criticism and our novels richer.

And this reminds me of one time, after I had run home to find the mashed potatoes gone, that I sat dejectedly in the house and realized, just as it began to rain, that I had left my book up in a tree. I had nothing else to read and was about to go out into the storm to retrieve it. The rain fell harder, and then harder, and as quickly as it began to rain, the drops turned to pellets of hail. Lightning flashed down around our little house, and there was no way that my parents would let me out.

I could barely sleep that night. I hoped that my book would make it through the storm, as if it were a fragile animal I had left tethered in the storm. When the morning was light I jumped up, pulled on my rubber boots, and ran outside. It was already hot. The

26

hail had melted and the air smelled of pinesap and crushed needles. I hurried to the tree and climbed up, my heart racing. I found my book exactly where I had left it. It was wet, and the cover had been torn in places by the hard-hitting hail. But it had survived. And, as a result of being allowed to feel the full force of such elemental fury (books are rarely allowed to feel anything but our hands and our eyes), a magic trick had taken place. No word had been altered or erased. None of the text had changed. There was still the same number of pages, but it was twice as thick as when I had last held it in my hands.

Smartberries

Readers will remember the pitch-perfect opening of Louise Erdrich's revolutionary first novel, *Love Medicine,* when June Kashpaw wanders off to die into the barren fields outside Williston, North Dakota.

June Kashpaw is intent on heading home, but the trip to the bus station becomes a bar seduction by a "mud engineer" named Andy. They drink, eat Easter eggs together at the bar, and, later, have a sexual fumble in his Silverado pickup truck before he passes out, and she decides to walk clear across the state of North Dakota wearing nothing but a windbreaker, slacks, and high-heel shoes.

The opening focuses very closely on June's body and the way she moves, "easy as a young girl on slim hard legs," on the Rigger Bar in which she meets her paramour, on the weather, which is overcast (but warm) for Easter weekend, all in all, on the tactile qualities of the stage set.[1] The third-person voice, which will be abandoned for the most part in the rest of the novel and replaced by revolving first-person narrators, is unhurried. The voice is patient, in control; the narrative eye wanders, but never very far past the surface. Only on page 4 does the voice veer toward the meaningful:

> "Ahhhhh," she said, surprised, almost in pain, "you got to be."
> "I got to be what, honeysuckle?" He tightened his arm around her slim shoulders. They were sitting in a booth with a few others, drinking Angel Wings. Her mouth, the lipstick darkly blurred now, tipped unevenly toward his.
> "You got to be different," she breathed.[2]

Then we learn that June feels fragile, like the eggs she's been eating, that her clothing is ripped and torn, that cruising bars for rig pigs like Andy is a sadly common fact of her adult life; she is a walking wreck.

And, after June and Andy park his truck along a back road for a quick and disappointing sexual exchange, walk is what she does. "Even when it started to snow" the novel tells us,

> she did not lose her sense of direction. Her feet grew numb, but she did not worry about the distance. The heavy winds couldn't blow her off course. She continued. Even when her heart clenched and her skin turned crackling cold it didn't matter, because the pure and naked part of her went on.
> The snow fell deeper that Easter than it had in forty years, but June walked over it like water and came home.[3]

Thus begins Erdrich's multigenerational tale of love and loss and survival. As the novel progresses we are introduced to a number of narrators—Marie Kashpaw, Lulu Lamartine, Nector Kashpaw, Albertine Johnson, Lipsha Morrisey—all related in one way or another, all telling their own stories, all trying to puzzle out two questions posited in the first chapter: why June died in the snow (which is never overtly answered), and who Lipsha's father and mother might be.

Modern readers, no doubt, feel as though they are receiving cultural treasures, some kind of artifact or sensibility that, if they are non-Indian, is different from their own and, if they are Indian, is a part of their tribal patrimony. Comments by critics tend to support this interpretation. Speaking of the structure of *Love Medicine*, the critic Hertha D. Sweet Wong claims that *Love Medicine*'s "multiple narrators confound conventional Western expectations of an autonomous protagonist, a dominant narrative voice, and a consistently chronological linear narrative."[4] Wong asserts that "Native American oral traditions have long reflected . . . polyvocality."[5] Wong enlists the help of Paula Gunn Allen, the most famous and most frequently quoted Native American literary critic, who goes so far as to say, "One useful social function of traditional tribal literature is its tendency to distribute value evenly among various elements, providing a model or pattern for egalitarian structuring of society as well as literature."[6] One wonders exactly what "elements" she is talking about, but then she provides the answer to our confusion by mournfully concluding that "egalitarian structures in either literature or society are not easily 'read' by hierarchically inclined westerners."[7] However, Allen's claim for equality among Indian parts is also true of the Homeric epics and echoes Auerbach's description of *The Odyssey's* machinery.[8]

Allan Chavkin, another leading critic of Native American fiction, makes the most strident claims for the inherent "culturalism" of Erdrich's writing. He suggests that the inclusion of both the "real" and the "unreal" or "supernatural" along with her "polyvocality" that "is ascribed to the magical realism of the postmodernists probably has its origin in Erdrich's Chippewa heritage."[9] It is alarming in a book dedicated to exploring the manifestation of cultural sensibilities in Native American literature that Chavkin feels compelled to include the modifier "probably." And if it does nothing else, the tentative link, the modest use of "probably," signifies that the relationship between prose and culture is "probably" a bit more difficult to identify than his claims suggest. At least it seems this way because while most critics of *Love Medicine* claim the book is somehow "Chippewa," they don't try very hard to prove it, and in the end, rely on (and largely misconstrue) what Erdrich herself has to say about it. While some readers have made comparisons between Erdrich's novels and Chaucer, Herman Melville, Cormac McCarthy, and Gabriel García Márquez, most discussions of *Love Medicine* focus on the elements readers take to be "authentically" Indian. Chavkin quotes Erdrich herself who says that *Love Medicine* reflects "Chippewa storytelling technique."[10] Case closed, evidently.

These are some of the critical claims made for the ways and means with which *Love Medicine* constructs itself. And, if the claims and the critics are not wholly wrong, they are at least missing what is most active, fascinating, and brilliant about Erdrich's masterpiece, and by extension, much of Native American literature. Let us allow Erdrich's prose to guide us in our exploration of her work.

In the first chapter of *Love Medicine,* "The World's Greatest Fishermen," months after June wanders off into the snow, her niece Albertine receives a letter from her mother telling her about June's death. After thinking over the news Albertine finally leaves Fargo and makes the trek back to the reservation. This unfolds over five pages. Three pages are dedicated to Albertine's thoughts about her father, mother, grandmother, uncles, and great-uncles. One page is given over to her drive north and west during which the narrative takes in the entire landscape and gradually focuses in on the reservation landscape itself. Finally she arrives in the middle of a conversation between her mother Zelda and her aunt Aurelia as they make potato salad and bake some pies.

All of it—the swirl of conversation, the quickly pulsing focus both narrowing in on pies or hand gestures and panning back out to include government Indian policy and family history—leaves the reader deliciously confused, weary, and like Albertine, ready to land someplace and to know what that place is. Erdrich doesn't create trust with the reader, she craftily makes us dependant on her for guidance. Then, King, June's son, arrives with his white girlfriend Lynette, their son King Junior, and Grandma and Grandpa Kashpaw—that is, Marie and Nector—and the vortex of backstory increases in speed and intensity. When Albertine thinks about her grandfather's mind and its rapidly disintegrating outlines she could very well be describing the reader's reaction to the book:

> Elusive, pregnant with history, his thoughts
> finned off and vanished. The same color as
> water. Grandpa shook his head, remembering
> dates with no events to go with them, names
> without faces, things that happened out of place
> and time. Or at least, it seemed that way . . .[11]

Toward evening, Gordie, June's on-and-off husband, and Eli, Nector's brother, show up. We are now twenty-seven pages into the novel. And then something seemingly minor happens. King, in a fit of drunken generosity, gives Eli his new baseball cap, which fuels the growing flames of anger between King and Lynette. Just when the argument between King and Lynette becomes physical, even violent, Gordie begins telling a joke: There was an Indian, a Frenchman, and a Norwegian. They were all in the French Revolution . . . After Gordie delivers the introduction to his joke while seated inside the house, Lynette, sensitive to jokes about Norwegians, heads outside. Then we cut to King and Lynette:

"There were these three. An Indian. A Frenchman. A Norwegian. They were all in the French Revolution. And they were all set for the guillotine, right? But when they put the Indian in there the blade just came halfway down and got stuck."

"Fuckin' bitch! Gimme the keys!" King screamed just outside the door. Gordie paused a moment. There was silence. He continued the joke.

"So they said it was the judgment of God. You can go, they said to the Indian. So the Indian got up and went. Then it was the Frenchman's turn. They put his neck in the vise and were all set to execute him! But it happened the same. The blade got stuck."

"Fuckin' bitch! Fuckin' bitch!" King shrieked again.[12]

This device, known as intercutting, works beautifully. It interrupts the swirl, the almost timeless flow of history and emotion, the seeming eternity of family dysfunction (where did it start? when will it end? what is the most important part to notice?) and gives the scene temporal and spatial rigidity. We finally have palpable conflict on which to rest our attention, that, when intercut with Gordie's joke, is frozen in time. The most notorious use of intercutting occurs in Gustave Flaubert's *Madame Bovary* during the agricultural fair when the story moves between three levels of action—the masses at the fair, the speechmaking officials on a raised

SMARTBERRIES

platform, and above them Rodolphe and Emma who watch everything as they prepare to make love for the first time. The narrative is timed so that Emma and Rodolphe articulate their desire just when the officials announce the manure exhibit. The effect is comic and wry and exemplifies Flaubert's use of structure as commentary. Flaubert made a necessity of form, he let his world work for him and in doing so preserved its naturalistic unity.

Erdrich's deployment of this device also creates a kind of unity, but a different kind. Intercutting freezes the novel in time, which makes it possible for both the characters inside the novel and the readers outside of it to analyze and inspect the situation. And, contrary to Paula Gunn Allen's claims stated previously, Erdrich's use of intercutting creates a delicious, heightened, and, indeed, foregrounded sense of the action.

If intercutting provides us with a framework—a way of focusing our attention on specific actions and specific consequences while preserving the feeling of flow and shift, then we still need something else. We need a vehicle for meaning, and Erdrich amply provides us with one: pies.

When Albertine arrives back home near the beginning of the chapter she smelled the "rich and browning piecrusts."[13] In defiance of temporality the pies move back in time, because on the next page, after the pies have been browning beautifully they are being patted and crimped by Zelda. "They were beautiful pies—rhubarb, wild Juneberry, apple, and

NATIVE AMERICAN FICTION: A USER'S MANUAL

gooseberry, all fruits preserved by Grandma Kashpaw or my mother or Aurelia."[14]

Two pages later Zelda "began to poke wheels of fork marks in the tops of the pies."[15] The pies continue baking while the story swoops back into family history and then forward into the present tense, until Albertine takes the last pie from the oven on page 22. The family sits down to eat. They argue. People get up from the table. Some propose a visit to June's grave. The novel is not hurried at all.

After King and Lynette fight, Albertine connects with Lipsha, and they lie down in a field and talk. Albertine falls asleep on the fieldedge and is awakened by the sound of a new round of violence. She rushes up the hill to the house and finds King trying to drown Lynette in the sink. Albertine tries to help her, but is beaten down by King. She stands up, and then she sees what he has done:

> All the pies were smashed. Torn open.
> Black juice bleeding through the crusts.
> Bits of jagged shells were stuck to the wall
> and some were turned completely upside
> down. Chunks of rhubarb were scraped
> across the floor. Meringue dripped from
> the towels.
> "The pies," I shrieked. "You goddamn
> sonofabitch, you broke the pies!"[16]

After King notices the damage he has done he quickly leaves. Lynette follows. They end up making love in the car parked on the driveway.

But Albertine cannot leave the pies alone. "Some-time that hour I got up," she tells us in the closing lines of the chapter,

> leaving the baby, and went into the kitchen.
> I spooned the fillings back into the crusts,
> married slabs of dough, smoothed over edges
> of crusts with a wetted finger, fit crimps to
> crimps and even fluff to fluff on top of berries
> or pudding. I worked carefully for over an
> hour. But once they smash there is no way
> to put them right.[17]

The prose arrangement is quite elegant. All the people in the house—Zelda, Aurelia, Eli, Nector, Gordie, King, Lynette, King Junior, and Lipsha—have been introduced and then have exited the stage, leaving a twist of half-understood passions and grudges in their wake. Albertine (arguably the sanest narrator and therefore the most reliable spokesperson for the whole) is left alone with the damaged pies. The pies, alone, spotlighted by the narrative focus they have received, carry the burden of meaning that all the human characters have left behind: they represent and symbolize those relationships. Regardless of how Wong and Allen would like it to be, there is no egalitarianism here, either among pies or among people.

As the novel progresses, we collect a number of symbols large and small that when taken together carry the book. Erdrich's ability to find that one thing that can stand in for all the rest is almost unequalled and only surpassed by Toni Morrison's symbolic strokes. For example, King's car becomes, literally, the vehicle through which Lipsha learns the secret of his mother's identity. When Dot knits the jumper for her soon-to-be-born baby, that little yarny outfit stands in for the burden of knowledge and the sometimes heavy bonds of family. And when Lipsha tries to unite Marie and Nector by making "medicine" out of two turkey hearts, those hearts, like the pies in the beginning of the book, stand in for the complex of relations, not only between people, but also between a past (cast as a cultural landscape) and the present (colored by the dominant society). When viewed closely the weight of meaning is unequally distributed, and this is how the novel creates its own sense—out of the tools provided by centuries of invention in Western literature.

It would appear that as much as critics would like *Love Medicine* to act out old-time traditional Indian techniques, it does not. Rather, it treats Native subjects with strikingly modern, or better, strikingly un-Indian, techniques. This is not to say anything about authenticity. The point of discussing Erdrich's use of symbol is to show how she makes her book work and to exercise a kind of interpretive attitude that makes understanding how the book works as pleasurable as the book itself.

The Myth of Polyvocality

In addition to the symbolic objects that Erdrich creates, the figurative language of the multiple narrators rests on the creation and manipulation of symbolic speech. For example, immediately after the close of the first chapter we get a chapter from the perspective of Marie Kashpaw (nee Lazarre) concerning events that took place fifty-seven years before the opening chapter, in 1934.

> So when I went there, I knew the dark fish must rise. Plumes of radiance had soldered on me. No reservation girl had ever prayed so hard. There was no use in trying to ignore me any longer. I was going up there on the hill with the black robe women. They were not any lighter than me. I was going up there to pray as good as they could. Because I don't have that much Indian blood. And they never thought they'd have a girl from this reservation as a saint they'd have to kneel to. But they'd have me. And I'd be carved in pure gold. With ruby lips. And my toenails would be little pink ocean shells, which they would have to stoop down off their high horse to kiss.[18]

In the span of thirteen sentences we are greeted with seven different instances of metaphoric language. We get "dark fish must rise" and "plumes of radiance" and "soldered" in the first two sentences. The next eight sentences are not only devoid of literary devices, but they also suggest an "uneducated" and "girlish" voice that has little grasp of grammar or syntax. And in the last three sentences of the paragraph we are once again bombarded by metaphoric images such as "I'd be carved in pure gold" and "ruby lips" and toenails that were "little pink ocean shells" and "high horse."

Erdrich's use of metaphor (mostly) and simile (somewhat), along with the larger symbolic moves of the novel are always perfectly accomplished. But what is worth noting is not their presence, rather, it is their placement. For example, the novel opens with a virtual absence of figurative language.

> The morning before Easter Sunday, June Kashpaw was walking down the clogged main street of oil boomtown Williston, North Dakota, killing time before the noon bus arrived that would take her home. She was a long-legged Chippewa woman, aged hard in every way except how she moved. Probably it was the way she moved, easy as a young girl on slim hard legs, that caught the eye of the man who rapped at her from inside the window of the Rigger Bar. He looked familiar, like a lot of people looked familiar, to her. She had seen so many come and go. He hooked his arm, inviting her to enter, and she did so without hesitation, thinking only that she might tip down one or two with him and then get her bags to meet the bus. She wanted, at least, to see if she actually knew him. Even through the watery glass she could see that he wasn't all that old and that his chest was thickly padded in dark red nylon and expensive down.[19]

All we have here is "killing time" (a construction so formulaic as to have lost status as metaphor), "easy as a young girl," which is simply a comparison of the usual variety, though apt in the case of June. Instead of the figurative first-person language we have a "naturalistic" or "realist" impulse guiding us through the opening sequence. It is hard-edged, natural, real, without affectation. As if a gritty life, a gritty reality, deserves gritty language. Erdrich creates a pleasurable parallel between her characters and their environment—but unlike the early Romantics and more like Raymond Carver, she adds an ironic flavor to her formula that saves her from empty or obvious allegory.

Such an opening, which suggests more Steinbeck than Faulkner, creates a reality in which the story will unfold. A reality filled with hard-luck women, dingy bars, and men in pickup trucks. Nothing onstage is extreme or fantastic, just quietly desperate. During the next six pages Erdrich uses only eight metaphors and similes, just one more than in the first paragraph of the second chapter. And these only occur when Erdrich is giving us a portrait of June's feelings and thoughts. Some of the first-person chapters begin with "straight" or colloquially inflected language in which the compound similes and metaphors are largely absent, while other chapters function similarly to Marie's first chapter. Interestingly, the three chapters that are the most imagistically loaded are, after "The World's Greatest Fishermen," the next three chapters, narrated in turn by Marie, Nector, and Lulu—the three chapters most remote in time, and most concerned with sexual and religious transformation. The metaphoric language unites disparate concerns, and it also adds a special flavor to these chapters. Or, better, it provides a metaphoric wash that is applied liberally over the past, giving it a special antique tint. The past becomes, not larger than life, but larger than *modern* life, which is crabbed and cramped and impoverished.

The function of symbol and symbolic language in *Love Medicine* is, to travel over only one textual bridge, like the use of symbol in early twentieth-century French poetry and fiction, to bridge the physical and metaphysical. Erdrich uses symbol to create a novel that is a novel about conversion both sexual and cultural. And while, of course, Erdrich manages to create characters who *seem* to speak and think differently [and, in certain ways, they do] they are all guided by the same consciousness; they all, underneath their different ways of speaking and despite the different poses they strike, function (psychologically, emotionally, and textually) the same way. All these chapters—whether they begin with a feverishly symbolic pitch like Marie's or end up there like Nector's—use a mixture of fact and fancy, a mixture of the figure and the figurative, to create its tensions and to resolve them. As such, *Love Medicine* is much more a book about language than it is about, or of, culture.

What does this suggest about how the novel is put together and how it functions? Clearly Erdrich is working in two modes, the naturalist and the symbolic. Erdrich begins her novel in the realist tradition and thereby reinforces what the reader might think of as both plausible and relevant. The language is easy, unself-conscious. It—like the original German realist poets of the nineteenth century—creates a matter-of-fact mood that is resigned and quietly discontented. That is, she recreates in language, at the sentence level, an easily recognizable Indian world: dismal, all too real, and desperate.

Erdrich's naturalist prose descriptions provide a gorgeous and necessary counterpoint to the intensity of the figuristic language she reserves for her characters and their emotions, and these descriptive passages signal and facilitate the transformations that take place in the characters. This becomes the guiding tension throughout the novel—a tension between resignation, the glum reality of reservation and Indian life, and the fantastic and colorful emotional landscapes that somehow manage to bloom there.

Applying many older Western literary techniques to a totally new set of subjects and circumstances creates a new kind of literary irony. For example, every one of the characters, the silly Lipsha and the serious Marie, engages in the classically Greek form of ironic self-deprecation. And the vast difference between the mean physical circumstances in which the characters find themselves and the rich symbolic speech in which they confess and the parade of objects (cars, pies, hand-knitted sweaters, and geese) to which they give symbolic significance creates, to use Cleanth Brooks's definition of irony, a "principle of structure." This irony reconciles, or at least contains, the cross-purposes, paradoxical aspects, ambiguous significance, and multiple agendas at work inside the novel. There is a wonderful irony here created between the language of thought and the language of event—the convening and pleaching of two different literary modes.

The use of figurative and symbolic speech and thought by the first-person narrators creates a mirage of sound. It gives the appearance of polyvocality when, in fact, all the characters share the same consciousness. If, for the moment, one ignores that each chapter is narrated by a character with a different identity, and instead focuses on the language they use, it is clear that all the first-person chapters use the same devices and same miniature structures. They all combine wild "emotional" language with sober "natural" description and in doing so mobilize one, sometimes two key symbols that are then collected together and built upon in subsequent chapters. Whether they begin or end with a plentitude of symbolistics they all reach for the Longinian sublime and for the place carved out by language for self-expression and self-discovery. There is no sense in any of the chapters that there are contested truths or contested versions of reality. All of our narrators (all of whom possess information we need) tell the different parts of the story. There is no overlap. Nor is there a sense, as there is in *Lolita* or *Pale Fire,* that the narrator or narrators are untrustworthy. Nor do *Love Medicine's* multiple narrators, like those in *The Sound and the Fury,* give us different realities, different impressions of the same reality. All the narrators of *The Sound and the Fury* speak and think differently. Not so with the narrators in *Love Medicine.* Not only do they think the same way, they speak to us the same way—each with the same reliance on metaphor and simile, the evocation of material symbol, and the lilting close of each of their chapters—but on different registers. The mirage effect is created by the use of symbol, not by differences in voice.

There are, within the limitations of the characters' experiences, contested facts. So if there is some kind of "polyvocality," it doesn't create a chorus so much as a round, each voice, with its own concerns and emotions, repeating (in structure and form) what has come before, with almost identical rhythms. Conflict and narrative tension do not arise from contested versions of events or from contested or variant voices, but from conflicting and interwoven modes.

The friction generated between these conflicting modes—naturalist and symbolic—creates, on an entirely different plane, a new kind of symbolism. If symbolism is, in its most basic sense, a device by which the writer makes one thing stand for another and thereby creates a relationship between those two things—then Erdrich's characters, who think and speak and narrate in symbolic, figurative language, are elevated and set in front of the dismal backdrop of Indian life. The characters become, in themselves, extractions, metaphors, and symbols of that experience.

The impetus for Erdrich's prose project does not differ from that of many other twentieth-century writers. She has the same desire to avoid naming a thing and seeks instead to suggest it. James Ruppert,

NATIVE AMERICAN FICTION: A USER'S MANUAL

another contemporary critic of Native American literature, writes,

> Native Americans unify the various levels
> of meaning that Western non-Natives tend
> to separate. . . . Erdrich merges this Native
> sense of multiple levels of meaning for each
> physical act with a powerful belief in the
> mystery of events. What begins on a physical
> level may start to take on a larger significance, but Erdrich leaves the connections
> mysterious.[20]

It is not clear what Ruppert is referring to when he says "levels of meaning" usually separated by Westerners. It is not clear because we were talking about literature not thought, and in written literature the task is almost always to suggest connections and cross-purposes and to create multiple and overlapping ideas clustered around and in events, objects, and characters. When Ruppert backs up his claim he does not do so by investigating Erdrich's language or style—he uses the example of Nector and Marie having sex on the trail to suggest that "what appears to be a moment of heedless lust" is really "an event that defines their lives."[21] One need not name all the physical events, purely physical events, in literature whose significance does not end up residing solely on the physical plane. Ruppert seems to be trying to suggest that symbol and ambiguity are somehow Indian and Indian alone. And as precious as symbolism and productive ambiguity are, there is nothing "Native" about either. What is maddening is the degree to which Ruppert's interpretation, which owes nothing to tribal language, tribal storytelling, or even to the long and brilliant life of the novel form itself and the inspiring variety of sources that came together to create modern literature, obscures the true genius of Erdrich's work.

Erdrich's fiction shares the same concerns as many other twentieth-century fictions. She brilliantly accomplishes what Mallarmé said good writing does:

> To name an object is largely to destroy poetic enjoyment, which comes from gradual divination or decrypting (unraveling of a mysterious scroll). The ideal is to suggest the object. It is the perfect use of this mystery which constitutes symbol. An object must be gradually evoked in order to show a state of soul; or else, choose an object and from it elicit a state of soul by means of a series of decodings.[22]

Erdrich's approach, while it has the same goal, is very much in opposition to that of writers like Hemingway or Carver with their maniacal adherence to the language of reality, with their stubborn insistence on addressing only the actual as a way to evoke the unnamable. The results of both approaches are the same: a painful distance between speech and event contained by a beautiful unifying field of language and sense.

The Sensibilities of Interpretation

Clearly a large gap exists between the sense of the novel and the sentiments that inform its interpretation. What must be dealt with is not a question of fraud or even of authorial identity. It is not a question of cultural dishonesty. It is a question of culture, expressed as a sentiment, as a wish. The cultural wish is even more glaring when we note that most of the scholars who claim *Love Medicine* performs culture—it is Ojibwe because it acts like Ojibwe people or Ojibwe storytelling or Ojibwe "thought"— don't bother to include or discuss Ojibwe stories either in English or in Ojibwe. We should. Erdrich herself has claimed that her "method" is a Chippewa narrative device. But since we have shown that she activates her novel using "Western" literary techniques, we should look closely at Ojibwe literature, namely Ojibwe oral performances of communally held stories, to see if we can find similar devices—symbolism, metaphor, stories told from different angles, etcetera. We should also see if we can find "polyvocality," and "multiple levels of meaning," and "equally valued elements," and all the other ways in which most critics claim Natives think and spin stories.

I've looked through the stacks of memory and piles of books for something that resembles a "Chippewa cycle of stories" without success. There are no performances recorded where several speakers take up the same topic and spin it out from different perspectives adding layers of truth and meaning or, at least, layers of approach. There *are* some stories however, that, for obvious reasons, have been told and retold over the years. Erdrich does not claim that *Love Medicine* or any of her other books function as truly traditional stories but since they are often taken as such we should look at some of them to see what points of comparison might exist. These stories are mostly incidental tales meant to entertain or teach, and their subject matter is funny and rude. Three of these Wenabozho stories stand out because they have been recorded over and over, and there are versions of these stories that have been performed and captured in the late nineteenth century, mid-twentieth century, and again more recently. These are *Wenabozho and the Ducks, Wenabozho and the Partridges,* and *Wenabozho and the Smartberries.*

Since much of the scholarship quoted in this article makes claims for traditional storytelling and cultural productions without either dissecting the language of the modern writing or investigating the rhetoric and sense of the original tribal stories, it might be helpful to look closely at one Ojibwe story. Here is *Wenabozho and the Smartberries* as told by Rose Foss, an elder from Mille Lacs Reservation in north central Minnesota:

> Megwaa babaamaazhagaamed
> Wenabozho, ezhi-nagishkawaad wiiji-
> anishinaaben. Ezhi-gagwejimigod,
> "Wenabozho, gegoo giwii-kagwejimin.
> Aaniin danaa giin wenji-nibwaakaayan?"

Wenabozho ezhi-nakwetawaad, "Aanish naa, nibwaakaaminensan apane nimiijinan."

"Aaniindi dash wendinaman iniw nibwaakaaminensan? Gaye niin indaa-gii-miijinan," odigoon iniw wiiji-anishinaaben. Wenabozho ezhi-nakwetawaad, "Ambe wiijiiwishin! Giga-waabanda'in wendinamaan." "Ahaaw. Giga-babaa-wiijiiwin."

Mii ezhi-izhaawaad imaa megwekob, Wenabozho wii-waabanda'aad ayaamagadinig iniw nibwaakaaminensan. Wenabozho giigido, "Mii omaa waaboozoo-miikanaang wii-mikamang iniw nibwaakaaminensan." "Oonh, mii na omaa?"

Wenabozho ezhi-maamiginang iniw waaboozoo-moowensan ezhi-ininamawaad owiijiiwaaganan. Ezhi-mamood a'aw bebaa-gikinoo'amawind, ezhi-zhakamod. Mii dash ezhi-ikidod, "Ishte! Waaboozoo-moowensan onow ingwana. Gaawiin nibwaakaaminensan aawanzinoon!" Wenabozho ezhi-nakwetawaad, "Enh, mii gwayak. Gaawiin nibwaakaaminensan aawanzinoon. Mii azhigwa gaye giin nibwaakaayan."[23]

And here is my translation:

While Wenabozho was walking along the lakeshore he met up with a fellow Indian. He asked him, "Wenabozho, I want to ask you something. How is it that you're so smart?"

Wenabozho answered him: "Look here, I always eat smartberries."

"Where do you get those smartberries? I should eat some, too," said Wenabozho's fellow traveler. Wenabozho answered, "Come with me. I will show you where I get them." "Okay. I'll go with you."

So they went over into the bush, so Wenabozho could show him where the smart-berries were. Wenabozho said, "Here next to the rabbit trail we'll find those smartberries." "Oh, here?"

Wenabozho collected those rabbit turds and handed them to his companion. The one going around being taught took them and popped them in his mouth. But then he said, "Ew! Those are rabbit turds! Those aren't smartberries!" Wenabozho replied, "Yes, you're right. Those aren't smartberries. Now you are smart, too."

The story was recorded again in 1997. This time the speaker was Collins Oakgrove, a native of Ponemah (as it's known in English, but more properly called Obaashing by those who live there) on the tip of Waaboozoo-Neyaashing on Red Lake Reservation. Oakgrove's version is a little bit longer than the one translated here. But there are no significant differences, except for a lazier, more indefinite approach that makes the solidity of the punch line, makes the extreme difference between story and reality, more definite.

Oakgrove begins by saying,

Aabiding giiwenh o'ow babaamaazhagaamed
a'aw Wenabozho enind, ogii-waabamaan
biidaasamosed wiijanishinaaben.[24]
[Once, as the story goes, Wenabozho,
as he is known, was meandering along the
lakeshore, and he saw a fellow Indian walking
toward him.]

I get the sense that Oakgrove is aware that his audience knows the story already. He knows we have
heard it before, and so he can proceed more slowly;
he can let the poor turd-eater wander and wonder
a bit longer before he pops the pellets in his mouth.
But the rest of the story is the same and, in fact, uses
the same exact words—*nibwaakaaminensan*, a noun
consisting of *nibwaakaa* (to be smart) and -*min* (a
morpheme meaning berry or pill) and the diminu-
tive and inanimate plural ending -*ensan*, as well as
the casual verbs *babaamaazhagaame* (to walk along-
shore), *nakwetaw* (to reply to someone), and so on.
The stories do not differ in structure—aimless wan-
dering, chance meeting, innocent question, cruel
trick, sudden realization, punch line—or event. All
versions also begin in the same place and are quite
clear about it, on the shore of a lake. The action then
moves from there to *megwekob* (the bush, or, literally, "the brush") where the lesson is learned. The set-
ting of the stories, uniform throughout all versions, is
worth noting. Why must they meet on the shores of
a lake? Why do they go to "the bush" as opposed to

SMARTBERRIES

mashkodeng (the prairie), or *noopiming* (in the deep woods)? You could say that a meeting along the lakeshore, which is open to the sky, is a place where such meetings usually take place in Ojibwe stories (as opposed to chance meetings on roads that so often occur in Greek myths and plays). The lakeshore suggests an innocent place, open, friendly. And then they go to "the bush," which evokes brush, small trees, and game trails. So "the bush" is different from "the deep woods" because there is a lot of action in "the bush" and yet it is not so remote, mysterious, and serious as "the deep woods." It is interesting to note that Erdrich begins her novel the same way, though the prairie is substituted for the lakeshore. June Kashpaw wanders out on the prairie and then, when the story resumes in Albertine's voice, the action moves from another section of prairie into the bush and then into the woods where Grandma lives.

But the similarities end here. I find it helpful, when explaining to my students the relationship between narrative shape and narrative effect, to make lists. It is possible to make a list of the things that Ojibwe stories like Wenabozho stories do and don't do:

- The first person is never used. In fact, there is not a single Wenabozho story that is narrated in the first person.
- The issue of motivation is conspicuously absent from the story. No one wonders why Wenabozho does what he does. Such mischief is actually his job.

- There is a complete lack of what can be seen as metaphor, simile, metonym, or implied comparison. The story is quite beautifully literal.
- There is no sense of "subjectivity" or "competing versions."
- The narratives are supremely stable. What happens, happens. And it happens in an orderly fashion.
- They exist outside of time. That is, when the story takes place is of absolutely no importance. It could have happened yesterday or three hundred years ago.
- They exist (for the most part) in indefinite relation to other Wenabozho stories. It does not matter which story is told first or which story occurs first in time. In fact, there is no way to tell if Wenabozho gave his friend "smartberries" before or after any of the other stories in which Wenabozho appears, and it doesn't matter.
- There is never a moment when the story shifts register. They have their own style, of course, their own unique pleasures. But there is no sense that there is tension between competing or pleached styles or modes: no war between realism and fantasy, no notion of magic realism that, by its very difference, comments on the reality that we inhabit.

Stories like *Wenabozho and the Smartberries* and the larger Ojibwe oral tradition are incredibly remote from *Love Medicine*'s structure, style, and content. This is not to say that *Love Medicine* is Indian or is not, just that the question is not important because the mode of production in *Love Medicine* is not cultural. But culture, as a *concept*, as an *idea* promoted by the characters, culture as a subject, is a very important part of the book. Ojibwe culture and the characters' obsession with it, is nowhere more apparent than in the 1993 edition of *Love Medicine*, which highlights cultural longing even more than the original version does. Characters, young and old—with the ease and melancholy of young, fin de siècle noblemen contemplating the wheeling of the heavens—reflect on culture in long, uninterrupted interior monologues, and such reflections are typically cast as reflections on Ojibwe language.

The first exchange about Indianness, occurs in the first chapter of the novel:

"Can you gimme a cigarette, Eli?" King asked.

"When you ask for a cigarette around here," said Gordie, "you don't say can I have a cigarette. You say *ciga swa?*"

"Them Michifs ask like that," Eli said. "You got to ask a real old-time Indian like me for the right words."[25]

Gordie, who sort of knows Ojibwe, or Mitchif (the Plains combination of Cree and French), tells King how to ask. Eli, who it is suggested definitely knows Ojibwe confirms what Gordie says. Yet, "ciga swa" (or *zagaswaa* as it is typically spelled) means "he smokes." The verb, uninflected, unmodified, does not fit the context. In no dialect does "ciga swa" mean "give me a smoke." The mistake is not a grammatical or idiomatic mistake that the characters would make. It would seem that for all their longing, the characters don't know what to say in their language and are much more adept at talking in English about it.

Ojibwe language, and the issue of translation that attends it, is even more important in Erdrich's later novels. For instance, two-thirds of the way through *The Antelope Wife,* two characters steal a German prisoner. What ensues is an amazing feat of cultural translation. The prisoner, who has been able to intuit that his life is in danger, makes an incredible effort to save his own life, though the only weapon he has is his cake-baking ability.

> *"Grüssen!"* the prisoner bowed. His voice was pie sweet and calm as toast. *"Was ist los? Wo sind wir?"*
>
> Nobody answered his words even though he next made known by signs—an imaginary scoop to his mouth, a washing motion on his rounded stomach—his meaning.
>
> *"Haben Sie hunger?"* he asked hopefully. *"Ich bin sehr gut Küchenchef."*
>
> "Mashkimood, mashkimood." Asin's attitude was close to panic. He wanted to put the bag over the boy's head. Because he had once been known as a careful and judicious old

man, the others had to wonder if there was something in the situation they just hadn't figured yet. The kitchen, a window shedding frail light on an old wooden table, the stove in the background of the room, the prisoner blinking.

"'Skimood!" Asin cried again, and Shawano picked up the gunny-sack uncertainly, ready to lower it back onto the porcupine man's head.

"Hit him! Hit him!" Asin now spoke in a low and threatful tone. At his command, everyone fell silent, considering. Yet it was apparent, also, that the old man was behaving in an extreme and uncharacteristic fashion.

"Why should we do that?" asked Pugweyan.

"It is the only way to satisfy the ghosts," Asin answered.

"Haben Sie alles hunger, bitte? Wenn Sie hunger haben, ich werde für sie ein Kuchen machen. Versuch mal, bitte." The prisoner asked his question, made his offer, modestly and pleasantly, though he seemed now in his wary poise to have understood the gravity of Asin's behavior. He seemed, in fact, to know that his life hung in the balance although Asin had spoken his cruel command in the old language. Not only that, but he suddenly, with a burst of enormous energy, tried again to make good on his offer, using peppy eating motions and rubbing his middle with more vigor.

One among the men, of the bear clan,
those always so eager for food, finally nodded.
"Why not?" said Bootch. "Let him prepare
his offering. We will test it and see if his sweet
cake can save his life."[26]

Two very strange things are going on here. First, the German is not translated, and the only help the reader is given is in the form of vague, if vigorous, stomach rubbing and eating gestures. Bootch, clearly the smartest of the bunch, knows, by dint of intuition that the German is talking about baking a cake. How did he know? It continues on the next page. "'Erdbeeren,' he said, softly, with mistaken and genuine sincerity. 'I fuck you thank you.'" His giftor responds: "'Gaween gego,' she said, *meaning it was nothing special.*"[27] (emphasis mine) Second, the Ojibwe, though much less complex, consisting of one word and a short phrase (as opposed to the compound sentences in German), is explained both contextually and in translation. The bizarre position of Ojibwe occurs elsewhere in *The Antelope Wife*: "My branch of the Ojibwa sticks to its anokee. *That word, which means work, is in our days of the week.*"[28] (emphasis mine) The German is not translated. Ojibwe is. This creates a textual inequality between German and Ojibwe, not to mention between Ojibwe and English; Ojibwe is neither fluid, like the English, nor densely cryptic, a site of strange meaning and difference, like the German.

Why is the German more or less left to be understood, while the Ojibwe is given special explanations?

After all, having an English "translation" following the Ojibwe text obviates the need for Ojibwe at all—the Ojibwe language is textually irrelevant; it does not communicate useful information nor does it engage in that other trick of language by withholding information or meaning.

When we look more closely, we see that Ojibwe crops up in *The Antelope Wife* in three contexts: as nouns, as proper nouns, and as expressions. In all three instances Ojibwe is subordinate to its English context and irrelevant to the complicated plot, story, and thematic development of the novel.

Roughly 90 percent of the Ojibwe words found in *The Antelope Wife* are nouns: *makak, ode'min, mashkimod, bakwezhigan,* and *nibi,* for example.* In these instances, even when they are not explained, they are situated within English syntactical constructions. One way this happens is by introducing Ojibwe words with English articles—the, a, an. The Ojibwe language, however, does not have articles. To write "the weyass," is to mean "*the the* meat." It is not unlike sitting down to dinner at what you've been told is an exclusive, expensive, and excellent French restaurant and noticing that the prime rib is served "with au jus."

Another syntactical concession in *The Antelope Wife,* but also in many other novels by Erdrich, is the

---

* I have, in this instance, not preserved the standardized spelling most commonly used with the Ojibwe language, popularly known as the double-vowel system.

use of locatives. In Ojibwe, prepositions such as into, at, on, and beside, are designated by adding a locative ending to the noun in question. Town is *odena*. *In* town, or *at* town; *oodenaang*. In *The Antelope Wife* Ojibwe place names are always introduced without regard to Ojibwe grammar or syntax. Again, to say, "I'm going to Gakaabikaang," is to say, "I am going *to to* Minneapolis."

Clearly, Ojibwe words have been lifted out of their own element and hosted in English, and not hosted very well. The expressions favored in the novel are particles that do make grammatical sense on their own and are the least obtrusive instance of Ojibwe in the text. *Gego, eya,* and *howah* are the most common and do little except signify the identity of the speaker. To be fair, it would be clumsy and strange to use Ojibwe-language-derived syntactical constructions when using Ojibwe words. Erdrich adheres to the most popular conventions that govern the use of foreign words in English. But as it is, the reader is left with sentiments about the Ojibwe language and instances in which Ojibwe functions as an ornament, not as a working part of the novel's machinery.

Ojibwe is a language dominated by verbs. One word count lists verbs as comprising 80 percent of the language. To see only two or three Ojibwe verbs in Erdrich's entire novel is thus striking. The closest thing to a conversation in Ojibwe, which occurs among a group of elder women on page 171, contains no verbs whatsoever. An incredibly beautiful, primarily "active" language is reduced to a few nouns, simple phrases, and the like. All of this has consequences. The language of *The Antelope Wife* and *Love Medicine* is not the Ojibwe language. Languages are systems of words and their representation used to construct relationships based on communication and noncommunication between people and communities. Much of what we see in Erdrich's novel are Ojibwe words. As with many other Native American novels, the use of lexical nuggets ends up feeling more like display, with language itself a museum piece. Even though Erdrich's use of Ojibwe has evolved since its inclusion in *Love Medicine,* the issue of language should stay with us. When many Native American languages are in the process of dying out it is vitally important to interrogate our use of those languages.

The longing for culture is linked to the project of self-recovery and self-discovery. The importance of "the old language" is the most obvious aspect of cultural longing in Erdrich's writing. The function of Ojibwe becomes especially interesting in *Love Medicine* when Marie Kashpaw is in labor, and Rushes Bear, aka Margaret Kashpaw, helps her through the ordeal:

> I tried to gather myself, to remember
> things. Each one was different. Each labor
> I had been through had its word, a help-
> ing word, one I could use like an instruc-
> tion to get me through. I searched my mind,
> let it play in the language. Perhaps because
> of Rushes Bear or because of the thought
> of Fleur, the word that finally came wasn't

English, but out of childhood, out of memory, an old word I had forgotten the use of, *Babaumawaebigowin.*

I knew it was a word that was spoken in a boat, but I could not think how, or when, or what it meant. It took a long time to repeat, to pronounce. Between times, the round syllables bobbed on my tongue. I began to lose track of where I was, in my absorption, and sometimes I saw myself as from a distance, floating calm, driven by long swells of waves.[29]

It's not surprising that that word *babaumawae-bigowin* was so hard for Marie to get her mind around. It would make little sense to her if she spoke Minnesota Ojibwe, even less sense if she spoke Mitchif. Contrary to what Marie believes or wants to believe, there is no morpheme that represents boat. *Babaam-* is a reduplicative prefix that suggests aimless motion, *-a-* is simply a connector, *-waeb* is a morpheme that suggests to use force or forcefully, *-iig,* water; while *-owin* is simply a suffix that changes a verb to a noun. Taken altogether and with the proper spelling, *babaamawaebigowin* suggests the aimless movement as marked by sound, of water; a disturbed surface perhaps.

But dim as her understanding should be, the word continues to help Marie:

Now I clung on to their voices, all I had, as they spoke to me in low tones, as they told me when to hold my breath and when to let it go.

I understood perfectly although they spoke
only in the old language. Once, someone used
my word. *Babaumawaebigowin,* and I understood that I was to let my body be driven by
the waves, like a boat to shore, like someone
swimming toward a very small light.[30]

The miracle of birth. Out of nothing comes a
complete understanding of a language foreign to
the character. And the word itself, taken from Basil
Johnston's *Ojibwe Language Lexicon for Beginners,*
would have been foreign to Rushes Bear or Nana-
push. Johnston and his dialect are local to Cape
Croker, near Detroit, Michigan. Ojibwe is a different
language from Mitchif, which is the language spoken
at Turtle Mountain Reservation in North Dakota—
the community and culture on which those in *Love
Medicine* are modeled. There is nothing in the word
to suggest the thoughts that occurred to Marie. No
sense of "body" or "boat" or "swimming" or "light."
In fact, the string of similes that Marie associates
with her "helping word" are all beautifully at home
in English, not in Ojibwe.

Strangely, the use of Ojibwe words—though done
seldom—highlights the longing for culture, not its
presence. It is longing because we don't long for something we already have. These scattered words play a
supporting role—always explained in English, always subordinate. All of the chapters are being told
to us, to the reader, in the "language of the character's mind." These chapters are confessionals. And
even if someone like Marie "started speaking the old

language, falling back through time to the words that Lazarres had used among themselves," it is not enough of a falling back to have her narrate her chapters in "the old language."[31] Marie says she is falling back into the old language, but her fall is *narrated* in English. She is falling back into the *idea* of Ojibwe language, not the language itself. Like convertibles and pies, language, and even the idea of culture, function as a symbol. It is the English language and the devices, tricks, modes, and traditions of Western literature, after all, that create the sense of the novel. The use of Ojibwe language and culture are only part of a beautiful array of symbols and metaphors that inform it.

But this is where *Love Medicine* becomes most fascinating. What we have in *Love Medicine* is a brilliant use of Western literary tactics that create, in gorgeous English prose, a portrait of culture. Instead of cultural desire what we have in *Love Medicine* is the desire for culture. Culture, as represented by Ojibwe words, is what the characters want. That they fetishize this or that word—and that those words don't communicate anything, rather they signify something— shows how culture is an idea that the characters don't possess but want to possess. This is a desire we see in many novels—*House Made of Dawn* by N. Scott Momaday, Leslie Silko's *Ceremony*, and James Welch's *Winter in the Blood* among them. The protagonists in all these stories are searching for cultural reconnection. *Love Medicine* is visiting common ground. Quite possibly, this is what makes *Love Medicine* a "Native American Novel." Self-recovery is achieved through cultural recovery, with English as the beautiful and terrible deficit the characters run in the course of their lives. The characters all speak to one another in English. They confess their lives (to us) in English. The very structure of the stories they tell, and their contents, are not only modern, they are "Western." The emotional syntax of the characters—their motivations, rationales, psychological divisions (think of childhood, adolescence, old age)—corresponds to standardized literary categories. Not only that, but, in moments of crisis such as childbirth, death, sex, and healing, the characters summon out of thin air not a culture that lives but an idea of culture that functions as a memory, not a reality. Culture is a paradigm the characters evoke but do not live by.

Love Medicine functions the same way. In moments of crisis—deep feeling or dire straits—it is the idea of culture that is summoned and serves to signify importance or intensity.

And perhaps the problem is this. Mii gaa-izhichigewaad ingiw wezhibi'igejig dibishkoo go ingiw mazina'iganiwi-anishinaabeg. In other words, our scholarship seems more like an extension of the characters' concerns rather than a serious attempt to understand how the book actually functions. A question we need to ask is why are we so desperate for the book to perform Ojibwe culture? Why do we want books to be culture or to pantomime it? What is gained by seeing *Love Medicine* or other Native American novels this way? Is it that, very unlike the characters inside the story, these books are an important, and sometimes the only, point of contact between readers (both Indian and white) and Indian culture and community? The fact is, this novel is not made up out of that Indian life. *Love Medicine* is created through a stunning array of literary techniques, sourced mostly from Western fiction. The real miracle is that with these foreign tools Erdrich convincingly suggests Ojibwe life. Be that as it may, just as Marie reaches—beyond her own understanding, beyond what is possible for her to understand—for some cultural notion that she can use, however inaccurately, to make sense of her own experience, so do we. We reach for a cultural understanding not present in the material to explain that material. And this is a testament to the book's power. So potent is it, so seductively does it evoke our inherited notions of Indian life, so beautifully is it wrought, that, magically, the concerns and concepts of the characters— these characters who long for a life unadulterated, for a life that is their own, of their own construction— have become our own. But to understand the book in our terms, not its terms—to ignore the ways in which it is actually constructed is dangerous for two reasons: by doing so we might save a book but we will destroy the literature, and if we don't look closely and carefully at what is actually in front of us then we are fated to learn the hard way and the price of knowledge is a lingering taste we'd rather not have.

It is so tempting for me to read *Love Medicine* as a cultural proof, and for a long time I did. The book is so beautiful, so powerful and new, it is hard not to try and beatify it. But to make it divine (and isn't that what we ask of culture today?) is to destroy its humanity. To treat it as culture is to destroy it as literature. If we insist on believing that *Love Medicine* is a cultural document and that we can reach an understanding of its delicious magic without looking at it as a literary production in relation to other literary products; if we really want to use notions derived from desire instead of from knowledge, then I suspect we've been on the side of the trail eating smartberries all along, but we just don't know it yet.

Lonely Wolf

A few years ago I had the honor of going to Finland to promote the Finnish edition of my second novel, *The Hiawatha*. Toward the end of my stay, after a dizzying week of interviews, readings, signings, and photo shoots, I gave a reading at a Helsinki bookstore. The place was crowded with attentive Finns. After the reading and after a dialogue with a noted scholar of Native American literature, I retreated to the book-signing station in the center of the bookstore. A line had already formed, and so I began chatting and signing. After a few "typical" Finns got their books signed, I looked up and saw a man who (I must admit) looked a lot more Indian than I do. He was tall and thin. His skin was dark, and he wore his graying hair in a long ponytail. When he spoke, his English was nearly perfect.

He said that he enjoyed the reading and discussion. I said thank you. He told me that he had been to a number of Indian reservations in the United States. I said that's very nice. I then reached out to take his copy of *The Hiawatha* so I could sign it. But the man stepped back and wouldn't let me touch the book. Instead, after shielding the text with his body, he handed me something else to sign instead. It was an 8 x 10 glossy portrait of him. He was seated astride a low stool and, with his hair in two long braids, he wore jeans and vest (Levis and cowhide), and cowboy boots (with impractical back-slung Mexican heels), and a black stovepipe hat that went out of style with real Indians sometime in the late nineteenth century. For some reason I still don't understand he was holding a very pretty sky blue electric guitar.

He leaned over the table and said, "Write it to Lonely Wolf."

I wasn't sure I had heard him correctly. "Who?" I asked. "What Wolf?"

"Lonely Wolf," he said.

The customer is always right, I said to myself and prepared to sign it. "To Lone Wolf. No problem."

"No. No. It's Lonely Wolf. That's my spirit name."

I was always taught to be polite and I figured that a small grammatical mistake shouldn't stand between the man and his real spirit name, so I said, "You mean Lone Wolf, don't you? Just Lone Wolf?"

"No. Lonely Wolf is my spirit name." He was getting upset. I didn't know if he had paid for his book yet.

"Sure. What the hell. Lonely Wolf it is."

I signed it, right across the top of his guitar.

~

Language can, alas, confound even the loneliest wolf. And I still think about him. I wonder how he's doing. I wonder if that really was his spirit name. I wonder if the language barrier has kept him from assuming his real spirit name. There is, after all, a big difference between being a lone wolf and feeling like a lonely wolf.

Whether or not he got his own name right, he is not alone. There are many people who want badly to be Indian no matter the difficulty. It is a widespread phenomenon. There are writers like the poet Red Hawk who take Indian names and seem to practice Indian beliefs. [In my mind's eye I can still replay a poetry reading given at Princeton by Red Hawk. I can see him, with his beard and bald head and robes, prancing around the Jimmy Stewart auditorium waving a turkey feather over an abalone shell in which smoldered Western sage and chanting the chorus to his poem.] There are also the nameless many, mostly sympathetic white people, who go on vision quests and go into sweat lodges, and find there, in those modern reinventions, some connection to the past. And there is also Shania Twain.

As an Ojibwe man I can tell you that there are many Ojibwes who wouldn't mind in the least if Shania Twain were Ojibwe, and there are as many, even now, who are willing to make her one. It was a day of great sadness when the world learned she was not Ojibwe. In the early days of her career, when few had heard of her, she told interviewers and said in her publicity material that she was Ojibwe by birth and that Shania meant "I'm On My Way." When her album *Come on Over* went multi-platinum and she was suddenly on everyone's radar, she had to confess: she wasn't Ojibwe by blood. Her stepfather was Ojibwe. "Shania" (a stage name at first) doesn't mean anything in Ojibwe, though again, there are many Ojibwes who are only too willing for obvious reasons to make it mean whatever she wants it to mean. One magazine profiler wrote that even though Shania wasn't Ojibwe by birth, she was so beautiful and her album had sold so well she was Ojibwe as far as he was concerned.

What are we supposed to do with all of this? Take the case of Ian Frazier, who got into a terrible disagreement with Sherman Alexie regarding his book *On the Rez*. Frazier asked a simple question: what's so bad about wanting to be Indian? Ignoring, for a moment, centuries of attempted genocide, followed (very strangely) by an immediate and overwhelming respect and desire for Indian ways, I suppose there is very little wrong with it. And if white people want to be Indian, I guess I don't care too much. Someone else's self-loathing is not terribly interesting to me— after all, I've got my own to worry about. It is too bad that the debate between Frazier and Alexie centered on whether or not Frazier had the right to write about Indians. A more productive exchange would have addressed the very thin and skewed research Frazier had done for the book: he only got to know one family well, interviewed white priests rather than Indian leaders, and must have felt so unprotected and vulnerable and out of his element that he clung to the few people who seemed to accept him—and in this, he is more Indian than he could possibly know. An even more productive exchange would have been about why and how Frazier thought he could be Indian, or "feel" Indian. It was a missed opportunity.

What is worth noting is the idea that it is *possible* to become Indian; that it is possible to access or assume an Indian identity—not to misrepresent yourself for gain or notoriety like Shania, but to actually think that you can and do possess an Indian spirit. What is worth thinking about is what this sentiment says about how Indianness is conceptualized.

The strangeness of the idea is even more striking if you insert other races and cultures into the same sentiment. I have an African spirit in me. I have a Chinese spirit. My given name is Jim Johnson, but my French spirit name is *Jacques LaGarde.* I have an American spirit.

Somewhere along the way—in the eighteenth century perhaps—Indians became associated with a very specific set of virtues. And then, at a later point Indians were perceived as having vanished. Or, if we hadn't disappeared entirely, we were no longer perceived as being pure. We were diluted by blood and experience. This, in the imagination, happens during the start of the reservation period (because of the qualities of pride and independence and . . .). Somehow the virtues have remained, though we are gone. And Indians and Indianness persist as ghosts persist: as hovering presences that can be evoked and appealed to, linked to life but separate from it, no longer a reality, or in reality. We became but an essence.

This essence is all pervasive. It has invaded Ian Frazier, Shania Twain, Red Hawk, and it exists in relation to them and to others as something that they can access if they know the right way to ask. Like the Spiritualists at the turn of the century, the idea is that if you do the right thing, provide the right chants or attitude, or have the help of spiritual professionals (in this case "authentic" Indians), you can gain access to the spirit. In both instances—the mesmerics in the nineteenth century and those with "Indian spirits" now—language is a pesky issue best left ignored. What is interesting is that in most of the cases of ouiji- and seance-induced communication with the other world, language was not a barrier. The spirits communicated in whatever language the listeners spoke, and the spirits (even if in life they had been illiterate) wrote in the language of the petitioners. It is easy to see that the spiritual program of the nineteenth century functions a lot like Indianness does in the twentieth and twenty-first centuries: the desire for a connection is far more important than the actual means or logic of that connection.

For those who want to be Indian, who have Indian spirits and spirit helpers and spirit names, Indianness is nothing more than a sensibility, an attitude or spiritual pose they strike, because nowhere in their self-concept or concept of Indianness is the idea that culture (in this case Indian culture) is lived through language and custom and community and history. For them, Indianness is beyond language.

Perhaps this is why Indians usually live in the imagination as images, as pictures, not as sounds, not in language. Perhaps this is why in order to be convincingly Indian it is only really necessary to look a certain way—Indian identity is largely a pantomime or a painting, or if it is a story, the volume has been turned down. This would explain the fantatical attention paid to skin color, mode of dress, hair length, and the size of one's belt buckle or the narrowness of the bolo tie. Perhaps this is why that Finnish man could be Lonely Wolf: he need only feel a certain way and then dress the part in order to convince himself. And perhaps this is also why Native literature is so often concerned with two seemingly different things: image and emotion.

Most novels written about and by Natives are visual documents—stories that craft sequences of images more than matrixes of human interactions; stories that if you were to do a word count would have much less dialogue and more physical description than most any other genre of literature. And wedded to these images are scenes of raw and deep emotion (think of the crying Indian in the commercial protesting pollution, or of Wind-In-His-Hair proclaiming his friendship atop a cliff as Kevin Costner rides into the future, or of those colonists dressed as Mohawks during the Boston Tea Party). Think of what Little Tree says about the song his grandmother sings to him: "Grandma began to hum a tune behind me and I knew it was Indian, and needed no words for its meaning to be clear . . ."[1] Or think of what Silko says about Pueblo storytelling: "Pueblo people are more concerned with story and communication and less concerned with a particular language . . . the particular language being spoken isn't as important as what the speaker is trying to say . . ."[2] I doubt that Pueblo-language activists, those who are desperately trying to keep their languages alive, would share this sentiment. And this sentiment is precisely the one that, years ago, birthed this precious bit of dialogue in *The Last of the Mohicans:* "Ugh," said Uncas.

To be fair, in life there might be many aspects of identity that are extra-lingual and extra-experiential. And while there might be things beyond language in life, there is nothing beyond language in literature. Literature is language. Yet we see the same logic informing our ideas of literature and criticism as I see in Lonely Wolf's self-portrait. There is the idea that Native literature, or literature written by Natives can perform culture . . . that, by appealing to the earth or to circular storytelling or by including myths and so on, our literature can channel that hovering, ghostly sensibility into our prose. It seems to me that we read Native literature the same way that those who want to be Indian read themselves: wishfully, hopefully, inaccurately, and, ultimately, by channeling ideas (not actualities) of Indian culture—the ghostly amino acids, those ethereal building blocks of life—into our interpretations and our work.

Plain Binoculars

Fools Crow begins in the year 1870 and focuses on the fortunes of a young Blackfeet Indian named White Man's Dog. The boy/man is unlucky in almost everything he does. He has no special hunting skills, no "medicine," no women, and no luck. Gradually, though, his fortunes begin to change. Through a series of interventions, both social and divine, his life comes into focus. He gains power and prestige and as one would hope, those two things confer upon him a beautiful wife and catapult him into the Blackfeet middle class. But this is not a happy story. Running parallel to White Man's Dog's growth (along with a host of changes he acquires his adult name, Fools Crow) is a growing sense of doom. The more of a man Fools Crow becomes, the more his way of life, his culture, is imperiled. Ironically, the greatest and most powerful gift that Fools Crow receives is the one gift that won't help him—foreknowledge. Or more accurately, vision: vision of the future that we, the readers, know waits for him and his kith. This is the bare outline of the story.

The nimbus of praise around Welch's masterpiece, however, doesn't so much surround the book as obscure it. Without fail, most critics of the book managed to praise this novel (and we have to remember that it IS a novel) for its accuracy. Other novels in other genres have been compared to "real life"—treated as transparencies held up to this or that historical or cultural vista—but few novels and certainly no other genres have been so burdened with the real as Native American novels. It should seem strange that a fantasy (all novels are fantasies) is praised for how faithful it is to life (the "silent sister" used to make sure that historical novels aren't cheating), but it doesn't *seem* strange. It doesn't seem strange that critics have said that this fantasy is the "closest we will ever come in literature to an understanding of what life was like for a western Indian," or that the "conceptual horizon" of *Fools Crow* "through which the reader must pass in this novel belongs to the traditional world of the Blackfeet"; or that reading *Fools Crow* is "like finding a lifestyle preserved for a century and reanimated for our benefit and education."[1] This false praise (false not because it isn't earnest and not because *Fools Crow* isn't a great book, but false because it is wrong) is indicative of how "authenticity" and "accuracy" overdetermine and overinflect the way we interpret Native American fiction.

To be sure, Welch wonderfully realizes the material culture, the stage props, of the particular area and the particular culture. The tools his characters use—bone scrapers, guns, knives, bladder-bags—are so finely drawn that we're is tempted to wipe them clean after we're done using them. He also renders

NATIVE AMERICAN FICTION: A USER'S MANUAL

the landscape stingingly present. No other writer I know has ever given so much life to the north-central plains of America.

But to praise, much less to analyze, *Fools Crow* on the basis of historical accuracy and cultural outsight (because the novel is supposed to be written from the inside out) is to miss Welch's genius altogether. There is a magic trick going on here, but it is not the magic of the hypnotist (who gets us to see with great clarity what has happened in our past). What we have here is the work of an illusionist who tricks us into seeing what is not there, makes us believe one thing is actually another. Or to put it more magically, Welch has not so much opened a window onto the past (to mix metaphors as appropriately as possible) as opened a mirror to the past; a mirror in which the reader's concept of self and other, past and present, Indian and white, are reflected along with the story itself.

∼

As evidence for the "pastness" or "otherness" (which usually amounts to the same thing) most reviewers and critics have pointed to Welch's language in *Fools Crow*. That language—spoken language, and language ostensibly spoken from the firm vantage of a specific culture—is highlighted and foregrounded in the opening paragraph where we are told:

> Now that the weather had changed, the moon of the falling leaves turned white in the blackening sky and White Man's Dog was restless.

He chewed the stick of dry meat and watched
Cold Maker gather his forces. The black
clouds moved in the north in circles, their
dance a slow deliberate fury. It was almost
night, and he looked back down into the flats
along the Two Medicine River. The lodges of
the Lone Eaters were illuminated by cooking
fires within. It was that time of evening when
even the dogs rest and the horses graze undis-
turbed along the grassy banks.[2]

We have a very strange mixture here of "culturally
derived" expressions such as "moon of falling leaves"
and "Cold Maker" embedded in idiomatically sump-
tuous modern prose. There is a play of contrasts between the white moon set in a "blackening sky" and
the personified clouds turning in circles, dancing in a
"slow deliberate fury."

The use of "literally" translated or etymologically
bare words (words with all their threads hanging
out) is meant to convey cultural otherness. Or, rather
than otherness, it is meant to communicate inside-
ness. Welch's use of this kind of Indian-English is not
confined only to narrative. It makes its presence felt
more strongly in dialogue.

"Haiya! Dog-lover! Have you seen a ghost?"
White Man's Dog stopped. In the dark
he saw a tall figure approach. It was Fast
Horse.
"Here, near-woman! I have some white

man's water to warm you up." Fast Horse
had his arm away from his body under his
robe. As he neared, his arm snaked out and
hit White Man's Dog in the belly. "I joke!" He
laughed. "I thought you needed some cheer
since you don't have a woman."[3]

Both of these excerpts—the first an example of
narrative prose and the second of dialogue—are supposed to introduce the reader to a world in which he
does not belong, to which he is an outsider. We are
supposed to experience the language as a translation
into English.

"Literal rendering" (the casting of Indian thought
through language) is at first limited to two significant
and signifying categories—those of cultural phe-
nomena on one hand and white material culture on
the other. "But the stars were distant and pitiless and
gathered their light within themselves. From somewhere far off he heard the hoot of an ears-far-apart."[4]
The use of "ears-far-apart" is used to suggest the *concept* of the owl, not merely the bird. The effect is arresting—we have to search the sentence for the object
and the key with which to unlock it; "hoot" provides
the answer. This kind of signing happens quite often
throughout the book—usually to describe animals.
There are "sticky-mouths" (black bears), "skunk-bears"
(wolverines), and "real bears" (grizzly bears). In addition to this kind of literal rendering—the Englishizing
of Blackfeet animal nouns—we have literal rendering
for concepts, too. Winter or snow is personified as

"Cold Maker," and a certain type of medicine man is known as a "many-faces man."

As previously mentioned, the same, or a similar kind of literal rendering of objects and nouns takes place in speech. There is an interesting exchange between White Man's Dog and Fast Horse after the two have been on a venture against the Crows. The raid was successful, but one of their party, Yellow Kidney, did not return. White Man's Dog thinks that Yellow Kidney is being held captive by the Cold Maker because Fast Horse made a promise to the spirits that he did not fulfill. "'I have come to tell you to fulfill your vows. The helping-to-eat moon is passing and soon it will be too late.'"[5] In this utterance two things are going on. First, we have the literal and conceptual phrase for the month of November (helping-to-eat-moon). To say "November" does not only communicate the sense of the concept that the characters might possess, it also begs a question of consciousness, and to use "November" would unwittingly place the characters in our world instead of theirs. Also, all of the characters speak in sentences. Full sentences. They speak courteously and completely. White Man's Dog has just overstepped his bounds—he has admonished someone his own age, someone who is not only his contemporary but who has been, through life, more successful than he has been. Yet Fast Horse (an impetuous, unthinking youth as his name would imply) responds by saying "'So you think I am incapable of keeping my word. You think Fast Horse has become a weakling, without honor.'"[6] He even refers to himself (like Jimmy on *Seinfeld*) in the third per-

NATIVE AMERICAN FICTION: A USER'S MANUAL

son. Why does he (and others) refer to himself in the third person? Or, better, where (in literature) have we seen this before?

Holding onto that thought for the time being, the poetic effect of Indian speech, the friction of diction, not unlike the use of "literal rendering," is beautiful and arresting. The way Fast Horse and the other characters in the novel speak is quite different from the casual speech of "real life" and also a departure from the "real language" of Coleridge and Whitman. The dialogue—starched, without much reliance on contractions, formal even—removes the characters from modern life, sets them aside and "back in time." And this asideness, this *perceived* distance, is done with wonderful effect, but beauty in this case in not allied with purpose. If this habit or aesthetic inclination is supposed to suggest an insider's view, then there is a real problem, one that begs a number of questions.

First, in the case of "literal rendering," we encounter the issue of consistency. In a novel like this, that is, one written in the naturalist tradition, the prose voice can bend without breaking as much as the voices of the characters. However, if the book itself, as Welch and everyone else claims, is written from inside out then one would expect that its directionality, its sense of the world, would remain constant. Yet in one paragraph we have literal rendering and then, a few pages later, we have the regular English word. To return to the opening, on page 5 we are told that White Man's Dog listens to the far-off hoot of an "ears-far-apart," yet 11 pages later we meet a principal character named "Owl Child." On page 6 we hear about a "wood-biter" and we get the word "beaver" on the very next page. These word pairs are scattered throughout the book—"stick-that-speaks-from-afar" and "rifle"—the list goes on. As such the narrative conventions of consistency, point of view, and voice are sacrificed for some other effect. That is, if the book "performs" from one point of view, a Blackfeet worldview, perspectives or understandings alien to such a perspective would be unavailable to either the characters or the third-person prose voice. But point of view is sacrificed at the altar of prose convention. The novel form and novelistic conventions require consistency *and* verisimilitude; adherence to point of view *and* the presence of variation. That *Fools Crow* breaks the first rule in favor of the second is a testament to the power that the rhetorical conventions of Indian speech forms (or what passes for Indian speech) have and show that the book is not a conversation occurring within a culture as much as it is a conversation between the material and the novel form. As such, the worldview expressed through language is not actual: it is adjectival.

What's even more telling is when and where Welch chooses to interpolate these "literal renderings" and when he sticks with the accepted word. For instance, a third of the way through the novel Fools Crow has a second dream about an animal that appeared in an earlier dream—the wolverine. When we first hear of the animal on page 56, it is called "Skunk Bear" in speech and then on the next page, almost immediately after it is referred to as a "wolverine" in the prose.[7] However, the distinction between prose and speech breaks down in a second dream.

> "It is good to see you again, brother," he said, "I have got myself caught again and there is no one around but you." (. . .)
> White Man's Dog released the animal for the second time.
> Skunk Bear felt of his parts and said, "All there. For a while, brother, I thought I was a shadow." Then he reached into his parfleche and took out a slender white stone. "For you, brother. You carry that with you when you go into battle, and you sing this song:
> *Wolverine is my brother, from Wolverine I take my courage,*
> *Wolverine is my brother, from Wolverine I take my strength,*
> *Wolverine walks with me*"[8]

What's interesting about this episode is that it is, in some ways, a culturally central type of experience, paradigmatic of an Indian conception of life and meaning—animal powers, dreams, power songs, and medicine—yet in the song the animal is called by its accepted English name, not the Blackfeet-inflected "literal rendering." One would think that in such a culturally charged atmosphere we would find conceptual language, not the plain language. Yet the value placed on language here is not of the cultural variety—here it is important that the language serve

PLAIN BINOCULARS

the structure of the experience. Culture is subordinated to prose form—clarity, poetic quality, the simplistic power of chant are all crucial to this moment. These are all narrative considerations. It would be impossible to recreate the dignity of the experience with the use of "skunk bear" in place of "wolverine." As in: "Skunk Bear is my brother, from Skunk Bear I take my courage." This kind of sacrifice—culture and concept laid aside in favor of flow and flavor—occurs throughout the book. It would be awkward to call Owl Child "Ears-Far-Apart-Child." It simply wouldn't do. It seems that whenever Welch trades "literal rendering" for "accepted language," he is bound to consider the rules of prose narrative more than he is obligated to stay faithful to "worldview." And in fact, "Skunk Bear" or "kills from afar" and the like are simply two among many adjectival constructions used to give the novel verisimilitude.

Nowhere is this clearer—this need to respect the rules of prose composition and to abandon (momentarily, to be sure) the so-called "cultural perspective" of the novel—than during moments of physical action. In the passage below an attack has just been carried out by Fast Horse, Owl Child, and the gang:

> Fast Horse caught the loose saddle horses,
> then got down off his own animal and picked
> up the weapons. One of the rifles was a many-
> shots gun. He wiped the mud from the barrel,
> then fired it in the air. It was a good find. He
> looked at the two men lying on the ground
> and saw that one of them was wearing a

cartridge belt over his canvas coat. As he bent down to loosen it he looked into the face. The eyes were wide open and blue. The whites were red with bursted blood. As he pulled the belt from beneath the man's body, he heard a long rattle from deep within the man's chest. He drew back and looked again at the eyes. He thought he saw a flicker and knelt close to the face. He looked deep in the sunlit blue of the eyes, searching for life, and was surprised how far into the eyes he could see. But the man lay still and there was no life in him. Fast Horse had thought he wanted to take the man's hair, but those blue sightless eyes spooked him.[9]

The only literally rendered word in the entire passage is "many-shots gun." Aside from that we are told, in crisp, concise language—in language that obeys and even exceeds the "rules" set out for action prose—about the deeds of the day, which are meant to communicate the very real, the color photograph of consequence. Nowhere does culture intrude on the lesson and very few adjectives (five by my count) are used to set the scene. Welch, master stylist that he is, is adhering to the rule that quick action requires quick prose. Economy, not culture, is the watchword in moments like these.

The "literal rendering" we see cannot possibly be the result of an insider's view. Native speakers—of Blackfeet, English, or any other language—are usually delightfully unaware of the etymological roots of the words they use. The question, of course, is not how language functions in real life. Real life is out of bounds here. Rather, the question is one of consciousness and register.

Fools Crow strives to recreate a world and a time, and to do so it uses the stage set of the American West—purple mountains and tall prairie grass, the cool of mountain hollows and the chill of northwesterly winds. The landscape and lifeways in the book are brilliantly deployed in order to concretize this world. They, like the feasts and ships and swords and armies and even the dogs of Homer's *Odyssey,* are presented for their own sake, with as much vigor as the people on the page possess. It is gorgeous. We are presented with a real world here. And, more than that, the Indians who populate that world are not only realistically drawn they are also drawn with realist tools. Unlike *Love Medicine,* we do not have many symbolist moves here. As such, the foreground and background are determined by the action and aspect of the characters and their situations, not by the theme or idea of the book. It is a world at ease with itself, seemingly complete. However, the "literal rendering" doesn't jive with this. Very few English speakers know, for example, that "halcyon" comes from the Greek for "kingfisher"—a harbinger of warm winds and therefore, of good times. And it would be preposterous to suggest that a white character in a novel would choose to say "kingfisher-brings-the-good-times-days" in order to communicate both his cultural centrality and the uniqueness of his culture.

NATIVE AMERICAN FICTION: A USER'S MANUAL

Fools Crow betrays a paradoxical self-consciousness; a sense of self *as other* that doesn't stem from the selves in the book. To put it another way: given the way they speak and the use of literal rendering, Fools Crow and his cohorts are as distant from themselves as they are from the moon.

~

This brings us to the oddest aspect of speech in *Fools Crow*. All the characters speak the same way—even the animal characters. "You see, seven, eight moons ago I became aware of an evil presence here in the Backbone," [says Raven].[10] And later, Fools Crow tries to calm his wife who is upset that her younger brother has been bitten by a wolf, by saying "'Sleep-bringer will visit soon. All warriors have bad dreams after battle. They will pass.'"[11] There is, in each instance, the same solemnity, the same dignity and rigid bearing. It is more or less impossible to imagine any of the characters at any time telling a joke that is actually funny. Each character speaks in sentences that are, for the most part, complete, discrete thoughts. (This is the same philosophy that guided Proust—it's just that the thoughts of his characters are much, much longer.) In every speech moment—regardless of class, age, gender, or even species—the characters speak the same way.

The only exception is when the "bad element" represented by Owl Child and Fast Horse speak, and their moral turpitude is represented by their reliance on the word "sonofabitch." One would expect a book "written from the inside out" would have its ear to the ground of the shifting registers of speech—conversational, ceremonial, age-specific, gender-inflected, legal, fiscal, and otherwise—but it doesn't. Think for a moment about the different kinds of English, the many different kinds of English we speak in an average day. The way we speak to our romantic partner is different from the way we speak to our children. The way we address a superior at work will be markedly different from the tone we take with a mail-order-catalog representative. Our manner toward a good friend from high school will be different from the one reserved for the chummy clerk at the corner store. In *Fools Crow* the language, the manner of address between people, barely changes. The modalities of speech in this novel are not determined by cultural contexts. There are differences, of course, just not between the characters or their contexts. The most important speech differences occur not in relation to the range of speech moments in the culture, but in the distance of "Indian" speech from English. The prose voice and the dialogue are arresting because they sound so different from our own English. And it is this distance that creates the semblance of difference. The same tricks are often used in movies. American actors playing Russians—here I am thinking of Harrison Ford's recent movie *K-19: The Widowmaker*—speak with Russian accents even though they are speaking English. The fur hat was enough. But the director was compelled to give Ford an accent, not because he would have had one in his home language, but because he felt it necessary to make a movie as though it were a translation. It's an ironic form of striptease: by putting on like accents and fur hats (as many strippers do) the characters are "shown" as more irreducibly other, thereby heightening the sense of peeking in, of watching something we don't often get to see.

The tone of the exchanges between the characters most clearly shows this habit of language. Early in the book, Heavy Shield Woman, whose husband Yellow Kidney has been captured in a raid against the Crows, had a dream that she must perform a ceremony in order to "pay the gods"—in effect ransoming her husband. She sits her children down and tells them:

> "Do you see that bowl of soup there?" All of the children looked. "That is for your father." One Spot looked up into her eyes, but she pulled him close against her breast. (. . .)
>
> "What is the task, Mother?" said Good Young Man.
>
> "I cannot tell you but you will learn soon. It is up to all the people to grant me the right to accomplish it. They will have to decide if I am fit."[12]

The dialogue between mother and children is stiff and formal. "What is the task?" asks her child. This simple, domestic exchange is for all intents and purposes seated on a butte, wrapped in a buffalo robe, staring off into the historic future. There is another exchange, late in the book, which would seem to exist on an entirely different register than family talk in the family lodge around the family fire—an exchange between Fools Crow (now mature, almost a leader in his own right) and a mythological god named Feather Woman. She is the agent of a new understanding, a new vision (new for Fools Crow anyway)—she will give him a glimpse of the future of his people. She, like some of the minor Greek gods, has sorrows and complications of her own. She was exiled from her godly paradise because she broke the rules against the digging of sacred turnips—not unlike Prosperpine and her pomegranate.

> "After a while I overcame my sorrow and gathered up my sack of turnips and digging stick and returned to Sun's lodge. Morning Star, my dear husband, looked into my eyes and knew what I had done. Moon exclaimed, 'You foolish girl, you have done the one thing you were not to do.' Soon Sun arrived home and Moon told him of my sin. He became very angry and told me I must leave his house, for I would never be happy there again. I would always miss my people. He gave me the sacred medicine bonnet and my digging stick. Then he wrapped Star Boy and me in an elkskin and sent us back to our people's world. (. . .)
>
> "Storytellers say that Spider Man let you down and you became a bright fire in the sky. The people thought it was a feeding star,

and when they found the spot it landed,
there were you and Star Boy. They say you
were never happy again, that you rejected
your people, that each dawn you would beg
Morning Star to take you back."[13]

Again, the register in which the dialogue takes place—like that of Heavy Shield Woman and her children—is formal. Thoughts are fully expressed. Communication takes place unhindered by personal history or individual traits and intelligence. In fact, when reading *Fools Crow* the reader never stops to ask whether or not a character is smart or stupid. The reason: intelligence and individuality are not important in this novel. The idea of fate replaces the notion of character. The shortcomings the characters do have (ego or anger) are plain to see and are communicated clearly: Fast Horse is fast, and he begins a reign of terror against the Blackfeet; Running Fisher commits adultery with his father's youngest wife and is exiled. Everything is laid bare and occurs on a conscious level. There are no secret agendas at work in the novel, and consciousness itself is communicated in copious direct discourse.

The speech of the characters—full, direct, with all their points sanded off, and stoic—is oddly reminiscent of the speech between other family pairs and between hero-types and the gods controlling their destinies in *The Odyssey*.

In the beginning of Chapter 5, "Nymph and Shipwreck," Calypso addresses Odysseus and says:

"No need, my unlucky one, to grieve here any longer,
no, don't waste your life away. Now I am willing,
heart and soul, to send you off at last. Come,
take bronze tools, cut your lengthy timbers,
make them into a broad-beamed raft
and top it off with a half-deck high enough
to sweep you free and clear on the misty seas.
And I myself will stock her with food and water,
ruddy wine to your taste—all to stave off hunger—
give you clothing, send you a stiff following wind
so you can reach your native country unharmed.
If only the gods are willing. They rule the vaulting
    skies.
They're stronger than I to plan and drive things
    home."

Long-enduring Odysseus shuddered at that
and broke out in a sharp flight of protest.
"Passage home? Never. Surely you're plotting
something else, goddess, urging me—in a raft—
to cross the ocean's mighty gulfs."[14]

The similarities between *The Odyssey* and *Fools
Crow* are immediately obvious. It is impossible not to
agree with Eric Auerbach when he describes Homer's
technique which is also, in part, Welch's technique, as
the use of copious direct discourse; the full expression of clean, well-defined emotional states; a kind
of narrative generosity that fully reveals both internal and external states wherein a dog, a tankard, a
shipwreck, and a homecoming are all equally repre-

sented; with the almost complete absence of symbol and secret second meanings.[15]

One could go even further and suggest that the "ornamental epithets" as Parry, one of the best commentators on *The Odyssey,* calls them, the "long, high-sounding labels that accompany every appearance of a hero, a place, or even a familiar object,"—which are present in *The Odyssey* as metrical stopgaps—have been reinvented and redeployed in *Fools Crow.*[16] But it's a trick once removed. These phrases such as "long-enduring Odysseus" and "sparkling-eyed Athena" and ships that are "swift" or "deep" or "well-benched" appear in *The Odyssey* as leftovers, remnants of the oral tradition, a way for an improvisational bard to stay true to the metrical confines of Greek hexameter. Over time, we must insist, these epithets have ceased to signal or function in terms of orality and are now firmly associated with epic writing much the way wagon wheels that crossed the plains have become coffee tables in suburban ramblers. These epithets, so singular, so unique, now signify "epicness" (epicosity?) in books, most notably books that can be considered historical fiction, like *Fools Crow.* Stories like these contain grand, heroic action, larger-than-life characters who possess a keen eye and an ignorance of the wheels of the fate. But stories like *The Odyssey* occur once removed because while there were undoubtedly oral performances of Odysseus' fate before it was written down, there is no spoken original for *Fools Crow.*

This is, in part, how the literal rendering and

stilted, register-less speech occurs in *Fools Crow*. But, of course, the novel nowhere tries to suggest orality or the idea of "performance." Epithets such as "ten sleeps" and "ears-far-apart" and "many-shots" and "white man's water" don't suggest speech as much as they suggest *The Odyssey* itself. Not *The Odyssey* as it might have seemed to its original audience. *Fools Crow* sounds like our modern ideas about *The Odyssey*: full of tragic action, steeped in significance, and most importantly, remote, ancient, the bearer of an ancient sensibility. This novel is not written from the inside out. Welch has not created an interior sensibility, and it is not a question of interior and exterior perspective but of creating the illusion of distance. The dialogue and diction does not create convincing emotional or cultural interiors, rather, by way of *The Odyssey*, *Fools Crow* creates cultural and historical distance.

Welch does not list Homer as a source. When interviewed about *Fools Crow* he said that when he wrote the book he thought mostly of how George Bird Grinnell told Blackfoot stories. But despite Welch's conscious model, *Fools Crow* does not mirror or mimic Grinnell's stories or style to any great degree.

Grinnell, most famous for his work as a naturalist (he accompanied Custer's 7th Cavalry on expeditions leading up to the Battle of the Little Bighorn) and a folklorist, was the author of numerous books on Western tribes, as well as the classic *American Duck Shooting*, was, along with Theodore Roosevelt, the founder of the Boone and Crockett Club, and helped start the Audubon Society. In 1896, he "helped" the

Blackfeet, at an all-time low—destitute and starving—to sign an agreement with the U.S. government wherein they relinquished their rights to the majority of their territory. That land later became Glacier National Park.

As for Grinnell's Indian stories, they don't read much like *Fools Crow.* They are simple and straightforward renderings of Blackfeet legends. "This happened long ago," begins Grinnell's version of "The Dog and the Root Digger."

> In those days the people were hungry.
> No buffalo could be found, no antelope were
> seen on the prairie. Grass grew in the trails
> where the elk and the deer used to travel.
> There was not even a rabbit in the brush.
> Then the people prayed, " Oh, Napi, help us
> now or we must die. The buffalo and the deer
> are gone. It is useless to kindle the morning
> fires; our arrows are useless to us; our knives
> remain in their sheaths."[17]

It could be said that the language of *Fools Crow* mirrors that of Grinnell's Indian stories in that, in both cases, they preserve the innocence and straightforward narration that have come to mark folklore; in each the characters are stable types that undergo some kind of transformation; in each there is an almost regal way in which the characters speak. But the similarities end there. And while Welch might have wanted *Fools Crow* to follow to Grinnell's examples, there is a vast divide between desire and reality. As for Grinnell, he was raised in Audubon Park, taught the classics by Audubon's widow, and matriculated at Yale where he received a classical education before working as a naturalist for the Peabody Museum and editing *Forest and Stream* for over thirty years. That Grinnell read and consumed Homer is a matter of fact. And, in his collection of Blackfeet myths he was able to connect the Blackfeet idea of the afterlife to Walter Scott's *Alice Brand: Lady of the Lake.*

What is fascinating is that *Fools Crow* is held up as an example of writing from the "inside" even though Welch claims as a model (though Grinnell is no actual model) a classically trained non-Blackfoot folklorist. [Ironically, Grinnell was praised in the same way that Welch's achievement has been praised, using almost the same language: "Of all the books written about Indians, none comes closer to their everyday life than Grinnell's classic monograph on the Cheyenne. Reading it, one can smell the buffalo grass and the wood fires, feel the heavy morning dew on the prairie."[18] The hyperbole is forgivable but misleading—I did not feel any dew when I read it but I did smell smoke: why, again, must Indian fiction re-create? Why not ask the question—why do these texts *seem* so real and *seem* to so accurately reflect life when they use such strange, plastic means to do so?]

What is perplexing is how the claims of a writer of Welch's magnitude and genius, by virtue of his subject and his own identity, have gone unchallenged. Intention is one thing, and performance is another. And *Fools Crow* performs in ways that might have escaped Welch altogether. Yes, it is important to hear from Welch how he *wanted Fools Crow* to "act" but it is more important to ask how *Fools Crow* actually acts. As readers, we must pay attention to intent and echo. This is both especially difficult and especially important to do in relation to Native writers and Native fictions, whose sometimes unsupportable claims (here I am thinking of Erdrich, but also of Silko, Momaday, Alexie, and the rest) have been given sovereign immunity more than they have been treated as sovereign. And whether Welch was aware of it or not, and despite his best intentions, what must have felt right to him, what modes made the most intuitive sense to him, even if he did not recognize them, were, tragically, the Homeric modes of truly great literature.

~

Fools Crow is related to *The Odyssey* by way of style and sense, and they share similar epic concerns, but the book has another, even closer, relative. And this is Welch's particular genius, and his most brilliant and lasting contribution to Native American literature. The characters in *Fools Crow* don't speak from the perspective of nineteenth-century Blackfeet culture. They don't suggest the culture of the plains during the last century. Rather, they suggest nineteenth-century *literature* about Indians. Welch's characters speak like the characters of Cooper, Simms, and Longfellow with what, in his introduction to the new translation of *Beowulf,* Seamus Heaney unforgivably calls the "Native American solemnity of utterance, as if they were announcing verdicts rather than making small talk."[19] Whether or not Welch intended to evoke Cooper's Indians, he intuited that the best and most convincing way to create a textual fantasy that takes place in the nineteenth century was to enlist other textual fantasies of that time and place.

In *The Last of the Mohicans,* if the Indian character doesn't speak English or French, then he is not allowed to speak at all, except for the very end when Chingachgook has a lengthy speech. Elsewhere Chingachgook and Uncas speak through action and with an occasional "ugh"—which can, and usually does, stand in for the entire range of thought. But when Indians do speak, and Magua is the most common speechifier, they speak in Indianized English. Late in the book—Duncan is in disguise and Uncas has been captured—Uncas's cruel captors ridicule him, ostensibly in Lanape:

> "Look you, Delaware!" she said, snapping her fingers in his face; "your nation is a race of women, and the hoe is better fitted to your hands than the gun! Your squaws are the mothers of deer; but if a bear, or a wild cat, or a serpent, were born among you, ye would flee! The Huron girls shall make you petticoats, and we will find you a husband."[20]

Leaving aside the issue of intelligibility (Duncan cannot understand Lenape and the action of the novel at this point is tied to the presence of white witnesses) and leaving aside also the issue of lexicon (do the Lenape really have a word for petticoats?), we still have to think about the overall quality of Indian speech, so much here like the speech in *Fools Crow:*

> "I promised him we would each bring
> him four of the Crow horses. It will go hard
> on us if we don't." Fast Horse stood quickly
> and pushed White Man's Dog over. "Now go
> to your father's lodge and dream of all those
> women you desire. With the Crow horses they
> will be yours and you won't have to mount the
> dogs."[21]

The full sentences, the arch tone, the solemn sexual joking, the heroic remove are there in both *The Last of the Mohicans* and *Fools Crow.* The speech in *Fools Crow* sounds more like the speech in *The Last of the Mohicans* than anything else—and this is wonderful. It is not a sin, after all, to write a book that, wittingly or unwittingly, recalls books of the past as long as the mistakes of the past aren't repeated. *The Last of the Mohicans* is full of cliché but *Fools Crow* is not because Welch is a much better writer than Cooper, not because he is Indian. Welch is also much smarter, because instead of writing a novel in which he tries to make his characters speak as they actually did, he creates a shortcut to his new, believable world by appealing to the rhetorical past rather than the actual past. He evokes the nineteenth century as it is imagined, not as it was, in order to convincingly create it anew.

∿

But Welch's language works only because there is a second, more secret device in play, and when taken with the nineteenth-century literary landscape—which poses (like the Road Runner's painted canyon wall suggesting the mist of distance and the winding road) as the "real" nineteenth century—these two lenses give us a wonderful illusion of depth. Radically, the second device is poised both inside and outside the text.

Fools Crow is on a "journey of self-discovery," which is bound up in the lives of his people. He is coming of age at the end of an age. Part of Fools Crow's education consists of war honors, another part of his adult self is developed from his increasing expertise as a healer. He even becomes sexually potent and lands an unlucky (but nonetheless beautiful) maiden while sidestepping the temptation to sleep with his father's third wife. But the real developments in Fools Crow's life come in the form of visions and dreams. These visions are not mystified or set off or aligned as verse. The otherworldly experiences that Fools Crow has aren't portrayed as being otherworldly at all. They are expected and normal, if not uncommon, a bit like getting admitted to an Ivy League school: rare but not rarefied. Fools Crow has many minor visions and dreams, and toward the end of the novel he has a major experience.

Fools Crow has gone off alone to see if he can summon a vision to help his people. White people increasingly threaten his village, there is no agreement between bands. This outer turmoil is replicated within his family; his younger brother was not able to say no to the temptation of his father's third wife and they are engaged in an incestuous love affair. Fools Crow meets his spirit helper and is guided into a dream world where he meets a mythological figure, Feather Woman. She shows him the future, represented by two things:

> he saw inside the lodges and he saw the agony
> of the sick ones, the grief of the mothers and
> fathers, the children, the old ones. And he
> saw the bundled bodies of the dead, slung
> across the painted horses being led from
> camp. He saw inside the lodges of all the
> Pikunis and he saw suffering and crying and
> wailing. He saw mothers mutilate themselves,
> men rush from lodge to lodge, clutching their
> young ones, the elders sending up their futile
> prayers.[22]

Fools Crow is seeing the future, or a version of it. What he sees is, for him, the iconic future (for us, it is our iconic past): the past future of disease, and devastation. But his vision doesn't end there. Next he sees the white soldiers, called "seizers."

> When the seizers reached the edge of the
> valley they rode up a wide gully and up to the
> short-grass prairie. Fools Crow put his hand
> to his mouth to muffle the cry that had begun
> in his throat. He recognized that gully. It was
> the one he had just ridden down on his black
> buffalo-runner. The seizers were traveling
> north to the country of the Pikunis.[23]

PLAIN BINOCULARS

Fools Crow has just seen the massacres, or the impending massacres of Blackfeet people at the hands of the U.S. Cavalry. But his vision wouldn't be complete without the third and most visually arresting vision:

> He searched around the Sweet Grass Hills, the Yellow River, the Shield-floated-away River, Snake Butte and Round Butte. But he did not find the blackhorns. He looked along the breaks north of the Big River, and he looked to the country of the Hard Gooseneck and the White Grass Butte, the Meat Strings. But there were no blackhorns. And there were no longlegs and no bighorns. There were no wags-his-tails or prairie-runners.[24]

The vision is complete—he has seen the three things by which Indian genocide has been defined. Disease. War. The disappearance of the buffalo. The reason why the vision is iconic as opposed to actual is that while disease, the massacre of the buffalo, and the massacres of Indians by U.S. troops did happen, and were terrible events, they have, over time and for modern readers, come to signify the past. These events, when taken together, have come to represent the fate of the plains Indians. For this reason alone *Fools Crow* is not a text written from the inside out—it is written from front (future) to back (past). Fools Crow has seen what the reader has known all along is waiting for him and his people. He has seen the unspoken threat, the smoke hanging in the air. He has seen what the readers have always known was coming. When Fools Crow wonders about whether he will receive war honors or if he will ever get laid, these become painful everyday gestures in an environment where everyday gestures no longer matter. This is the same technique used to breathe new life into love stories. The movie *Titanic* does this wonderfully if a bit manipulatively. The characters are, of course, totally unaware that their ship is about to hit an iceberg. But the audience knows full well that the ship will sink before the evening's through. The certain death, the terrible loss of life, lends greater poignancy to the love story, not just because they won't get to live happily ever after (most love stories now preclude this), but because *we know* in advance that they will not live happily ever after.

This begs an issue of perspective—Fools Crow's and the reader's. All along he has been approaching our perspective, gradually coming closer to our modern understanding of the past. Fools Crow is now more like the reader than he was at the beginning of the book, and this is where the narrative tension, the play of comparison, rests. Fools Crow's vision literalizes the prestocked ideas with which the reader approaches the text—destruction and continuance. Instead of symbol and internal tensions between people (as we have in Erdrich, say), we have a book that constructs meaning out of symbolic perspectives. The tension in the novel is a result of split vision: the innocent and uncomprehending struggle seen from inside the culture and a fate waiting for the people in the future as seen from outside their time and experience.

Thomas Mann might well have been speaking about this book in his forward to his own, *The Magic Mountain:*

> for stories, as histories, must be past, and
> the further past, one might say, the better
> for them as stories and for the storyteller,
> that conjurer who murmurs in past tenses.
> But the problem with our story, as also with
> many people nowadays and, indeed, not the
> least with those who tell stories, is this: it is
> much older than its years, its datedness is not
> to be measured in days, nor the burden of
> age weighing upon it to be counted by orbits
> around the sun; in a word, it does not actually
> owe its pastness to *time*—an assertion that is
> itself intended as a passing reference, an allu-
> sion, to the problematic and uniquely double
> nature of that mysterious element.
>   But let us not intentionally obscure a clear
> state of affairs: the extraordinary pastness of
> our story results from its having taken place
> *before* a certain turning point, on the far side
> of a rift that has cut deeply through our lives
> and consciousness.[25]

Mann is referring to WWI, but holocaust is ho-locaust. And the "divide," the "far side" that Welch evokes, which contains our sense of what Fools Crow's future might be, is in part what creates the sense of movement, of inevitability, of time. Welch, arguably the bravest and most experimental of Native American novelists, came up against one of the most difficult and obdurate aspects of the enterprise of imagining the Indian: it is excruciatingly difficult to create fully realized Indian characters who exist in their language, on the other side of the divide of holocaust and colonialism; characters who have not yet stooped to English. Every other Native American novel, in order to overcome the difficult task of creating Indians in English, has characters who are distant from their cultures and themselves, and the novels describe a process of reaching back. How then, does one imagine a past where English has no purchase? How does one imagine it successfully?

The interpretive task before the reader when reading this book is linked to the task of reading many other Native fictions: how to make sense of material that looks cultural or is Indianized, whether it appears as speech or myth or history. In this case, to situate this novel inside the culture is to ignore the responsibility vested in the reader to interpret. And it is also to ignore what is most amazing about Welch's supreme accomplishment. When we combine a twentieth-century perspective on nineteenth-century Indian history with the eighteenth-century Cooperspeak of the characters we have an amazingly present and delicate web of sense being spun for us, not with the strands of culture but with the silk of language.

How to Hate/Love an Indian

The following text was printed as an advertisement in a South Dakota newspaper in the fall of 1999.

Dear South Dakota Hunters:

The 1999 Big Game hunting season in the state of South Dakota has been canceled due to shortages of Deer, Turkey, Elk and Antelope. However, this does not mean there will be no hunting. In the place of the big game animals this year we will have open season on the Sioux Reservations. This will entail the hunting of Americans Worthless Slounis Pyutus, commonly known as "Worthless Red Bastards, Dog Eaters, Gut Eaters, Prairie Niggers and F . . . . Indians." This year from 1999–2000 will be an open season, as the f . . . . . indians [sic] must be thinned out every two to three years.

It will be Unlawful to:
- Hunt in a party of more than 150 persons
- Use more than 35 bloodthirsty, rabid hunting dogs
- Shoot in a public tavern (Bullet may ricochet and hit civilized white people)
- Shoot an Indian sleeping on the sidewalk

Trapping Regulations

- Traps may not be set within 15 feet of a liquor store
- Traps may not be baited with Muscatel, Lysol, rubbing alcohol or food stamps
- All traps must have at least 120 lb. spring strength and have a jaw spread of at least 5' 3"

Other rules and regulations:

- Shooting length-wide in a welfare line is prohibited
- It will be unlawful to possess a road-kill-Indian, however, special road-kill permits shall be issued to people with semi-tractor trailers and one-ton pick-up trucks.
- With such a permit you may bait the highway with muscatel [sic], Lysol, rubbing alcohol or food stamps

How to Know When an Indian is in You [sic] Area

- Disposable diapers litter the street
- Large lines in front of the welfare office and for free cheese
- Trails of empty wine bottles leading from the city parks to all city alleys
- Empty books of food stamps thrown all over
- Car-loads of Indian children waiting outside liquor stores

Remember limit is ten (10) per day
Possession of limit: Forty (40)

Good hunting!

It may come as a surprise to many that Indian hating is such a refined sport. For most people who have little contact with us, Indians are just a pleasing idea, and however inaccurate their thinking might be, what thinking occurs is flattering. For many of the white people living near our reservations we are no less an idea—proximity might breed contempt but it does not necessarily breed familiarity—but their idea of us is oftentimes less than flattering.

What are perplexing are the *reasons* for *hating* us. It seems to me that we are not, for example, hated for the same reason that Mexican, Central and South American, and Southeast Asian immigrants are hated. They are hated by those who hate because, according to the propaganda, they are "taking all the jobs." We are also not disliked because we are feared in the way urban African Americans are often feared: as unpredictable threats to life and property, circling the city waters like sharks, ready to snatch and consume any vulnerable thing. We are not disliked for the same reason that North African immigrants often are—seemingly so alien and insular as to preclude any kind of understanding.

We are, I think, hated because we are perceived as not living up to our potential, because we are perceived as being decrepit, broken. This is what the newspaper ad declaring Indian hunting season seems to suggest. The writer or writers mobilize stereotypes. We are portrayed as not just drunk and poor, but, and this is what is so upsetting to the rednecks, but as *publicly* drunk and *publicly* poor. Stereotypes, contrary to popular thought, are usually very refined. All the stereotypes in the newspaper ad are related to our difficulties. In particular, they are related to our self-inflicted traumas. We are hated for our own self-hatred.

∼

Uninformed Indian love often draws on the same things as Indian hate. For the very same reasons hate flourishes—the hardships of poverty, alcoholism, and unemployment—love survives. And there is a kind of mathematical formula that we could come up with, with an x/y axis that charts how hate flourishes close to us and love grows in proportion to how far away the lover is from the beloved (it is no accident that Indians are loved most in Europe and Japan). This love is based on the same tension between promise and ruin. Those who love with that particular kind of admiration that is a blend of awe and familiarity, of pity and guilt, do so because commiserating feels good. And they love us because they have been taught that we possess certain key virtues that function as antidotes to the poisons of Western civilization. Our perceived virtues are closely tied to white guilt—virtues only because they speak to that guilt and point out the failings of Western cultures. We are, according to many, near the earth, natural-born conservationists, nonmaterialistic (which is a great benefit when you're too poor to own very much), egalitarian, and unpretentious (only those who have never been to the Gathering of Nations could believe this one). It is almost impossible for many to imagine some aspects of our actual Native cultures in which cruelty was praised, revenge was elevated to the level of art, where having the most was a very good thing, and being powerful was the ultimate end.

After all, it doesn't seem necessary to have a true command of our culture and history to love us, because love, like hate, is based on an *idea* of us. In the past, we regularly set large forest fires to increase the buffalo range, or nearly trapped the beaver to extinction, or massacred buffalo by the thousands (long before the white man showed up) just for their tongues and humps, and irrigated the southwest to the point of toxic salination. But our admirers don't need to know that, and in fact, don't want to know—they want to see us as the embodiment of what they are not, as possessing the virtues they desperately want.

For our haters—and as much as we complain about those who fetishize us we do appreciate their attention more than we appreciate that of racists—their hate is based on the same ideal of Indian consciousness. Their hate feels, to me, largely linked to how the Indians they think they know are not like the Indians of yesteryear, as our historical cultures are imagined. We are often perceived as not being like our ancestors. Where is our conservationist appeal when we litter? Where is that oft-evoked Indian pride when we rely on welfare and WIC? It is astounding how we can fight for our lives and then be hated for the fact that we have won at great cost.

It seems to me that in order to get anywhere, both those who love us and those who hate us should take a long, discerning look at our history and our literatures and quit treating Indians as a playground for the imagination; as the ground on which the emotions they have been trained to have (love, hate, respect, disdain . . .) are let loose to play. Or maybe that's the point: we are inconsequential, beside the point of daily life. Maybe that's why people *can* love and hate us so much. They give themselves permission to practice their emotions on us because we exist in a zero-gravity atmosphere of consequence. What part of the social order is disrupted by either hating or loving us? Those who know us, and those who don't, are safe to practice their idealism—ideal love and ideal hate—because it costs them nothing. Yes, it is all too safe to practice on us, to express oneself through us and our predicament. It is not necessary (and this is the root of our appeal) to be informed, actually informed, about our realities.

The Myth of Myth

Perhaps no novel has had a more profound impact on Native American literature than Leslie Marmon Silko's *Ceremony*. No matter what standard or rules of classification—such as dislocation, search for self, the importance of landscape, the use of traditional materials, "nonlinear" structure, the apparent *bricolage* of "traditional" and "Western" modes of storytelling—one wishes to use to define Native American literature, they all have, if not their root, then their best defense, in *Ceremony*.

Ceremony is, for the most part, set on and around the Laguna Pueblo just to the west of Albuquerque, New Mexico. The time period: the 1930s through the 1940s. The novel opens after the main character, Tayo, has returned home from WWII. Tayo is in a bad way—he can't sleep. When he does manage to nod off he has nightmares. In what becomes the physical signature for psychic distress he sweats continually and can't keep his food down. Tayo's trauma seems to stem from the war. But that is only part of the problem. Confusion itself is the enemy in the opening pages:

He could feel it inside his skull—the tension
of little threads being pulled and how it was
with tangled things, things tied together,
and as he tried to pull them apart and rewind
them into their places, they snagged and
tangled even more. So Tayo had to sweat
though those nights when thoughts became
entangled; he had to sweat to think of something that wasn't unraveled or tied in knots to
the past—something that existed by itself . . . [1]

While confusion and subsequent narrative order-
ing have been the mark of modern fiction since the
turn of the century—such works as *Remembrance of
Things Past*, *The Magic Mountain*, *Confessions of Zeno*,
and *Hunger* come to mind—Silko manages to give
the theme a particularly Native flavor. It becomes
clear that Tayo's trauma is longstanding and has its
source in something other than the war. In a search
for an explanation for his sickness, Tayo makes a visit
to the white doctors who misdiagnose Tayo's ailment
as post-traumatic shock. But Tayo knows better. "'It's
more than that. I can feel it. It's been going on for a
long time.'"[2]

What Tayo intuits, and then the novel explores, is
that his suffering is a manifestation of a much larger,
more diffuse world-sickness. Ultimately Tayo must
find links between his predicament and the more
general cultural sickness that has infected the modern world and that has its roots in the long sordid
history of Indian/white relationships. The novel has
two plot lines: Tayo must do some detective work to

understand his illness, and then he must search for a cure.

As the novel unfolds and his problems come into focus, Tayo makes various attempts at healing. These "healing moments" and the tests that always follow closely on healing's heels are what structure the novel. The healing episodes and the tests are linked to myths that are scattered through its pages. So it is crucial, if we are to understand the use of myth and how culture functions in the book, to see how the novel works by creating a problem, a search, and a cure.

Sickness

What makes the novel so difficult to describe is how Tayo's search for the true nature of his sickness runs alongside his search for various cures. The novel moves from confusion to order. First, confusion.

Ceremony opens with Tayo caught in a fever of confusion, specifically, a confusion of voices:

Tayo didn't sleep well that night. He tossed in the old iron bed, and the coiled springs kept squeaking even after he lay still again, calling up humid dreams of black night and loud voices rolling him over and over again like debris caught in a flood. Tonight the singing had come first, squeaking out of the iron bed, a man singing in Spanish, the melody of a familiar love song, two words again and again, *"Y volveré."* Sometimes the Japanese voices came first, angry and loud, pushing the song far away, and then he could hear the shift in his dreaming, like a slight afternoon wind changing its direction, coming less and less from the south, moving into the west, and the voices would become Laguna voices, and he could hear Uncle Josiah calling to him, Josiah bringing him the fever medicine when he had been sick a long time ago.[3]

Silko expertly weaves together a number of strands in these opening lines. She manages to hint at the presence and importance of water, both to the New Mexican landscape and to the Pacific theatre; to suggest a further link between the Japanese and the Pueblo community from which Tayo comes [and, incidentally, Spanish (which in *Ceremony* is the language of passion)]; and to thematize the pressure and importance of language and the process of articulation itself. All of this in the first paragraph.

After this artful opening, Silko begins investigating all these issues—we can't really call them themes because rain, language, WWII, and Tayo's childhood are actual, not aesthetic—as if dissecting a tumor and following the muscles, veins, and nerves that extend into the body of the novel.

First, Silko explores Tayo's mental collapse in the jungles of Asia where, exhausted and possibly malarial (but possibly something else), Tayo confuses a dead Japanese solider with his uncle Josiah. He thinks he has killed his uncle. Tayo's cousin, Rocky, tries to set Tayo straight, but is unable to do so. Silko's narrative then emerges from the foliage of the jungle and comes back to the American Southwest, which has suffered from drought since Tayo left for the war. Almost immediately, we are back in the jungle. We learn that Rocky has been wounded, Tayo has been taken prisoner. He and the corporal mentioned before are forced to carry Rocky's body in a makeshift stretcher. For Tayo, the rain is a curse—it makes carrying and caring for Rocky difficult. He slips and slides and falls. We are only a few pages into the novel, but the issues that Silko laid out in the first paragraph are coming quickly into focus. The links are becoming more obvious to the reader. Tayo blames himself for Rocky's death and for the drought that has afflicted his Laguna home for six years: "So he had prayed the rain away, and for the sixth year it was dry; the grass turned yellow and it did not grow. . . . and he got the choking in his throat again, and he cried for all of them, and for what he had done."[4]

So we have a mixture of traumas—Rocky's death, Tayo's compound guilt, and the drought that may or may not be Tayo's fault. Silko has, in a few short pages, created three levels of conflict, three grounds, on which the novel is built: the recent past (WWII), the present (drought and psychic wounds), and, a barely hinted at, suggested but not named, and more widespread sickness.

The action resumes, moving between Tayo's return to the months that follow and is mostly concerned with Tayo's quest for healing amidst an escalation of violence around him. The first attempt at healing occurs shortly after his return home when Tayo's grandmother tries to arrange for a medicine man of the old variety (tradition-bound, culturally central) to visit Tayo. The old man, Ku'oosh, tries the "old" ways of healing. But they don't seem to work. Ku'oosh hesitates, he is unable to help Tayo:

> But the old man would not have believed
> white warfare—killing across great distances
> without knowing who or how many had died.
> It was all too alien to comprehend, the mor-
> tars and big guns; and even if he could have
> taken the old man to see the target areas, even
> if he could have led him through the fallen
> jungle trees and muddy craters of torn earth
> to show him the dead, the old man would not
> have believed anything so monstrous.[5]

After mobilizing the reader's expectation that modern war creates unavoidable psychic trauma—the novel was written during the last years of the Vietnam War—and then by creating a cure that ends up being no cure, Silko has drawn the reader in. Only now, we realize, is the problem much larger than the recent war, or Tayo's personal troubles, or his outsider/insider status as a mixed blood. This brings us—after collecting Tayo's troubled childhood, his loving but complicated relationship with his uncle, and his recent troubles with war buddies like Emo and Harley—to his second attempt at healing.

He visits a mixed-blood Navajo healer named Betonie on the outskirts of Gallup, New Mexico. Betonie seems an unlikely healer from the start—too modern and too disconnected at the same time. Tayo has doubts that are only heightened when he notices that Betonie's hogan is filled with the ephemera of Western culture—bags of clothes, boxes of paper, and stacks of phone books. Tayo is confused and distrustful of the syncretic nature of Betonie's persona and his personal belongings. Soon, however, Tayo begins to talk to and to trust Betonie. And by virtue of his syncretism, the healer validates both Tayo's gory ennui and the structure of the novel itself—which moves back and forth in time collecting problems and illnesses as it goes (Tayo's problems, the drought, Rocky's death, the homeless Indians outside of Gallup)—when he has an epiphany halfway through Tayo's cure:

> The old man had jumped up. He was walking around the fire pit, moving behind Tayo as he went around. He was excited, and from time to time he would say something to himself in Navajo. (. . .)
>
> "I'm beginning to see something," he said with his eyes closed, "yes. Something very important."
>
> The room was cooler than before. The light from the opening in the roof was becoming diffuse and gray. It was sundown. Betonie pointed a finger at him.
>
> "This has been going on for a long long time. They will try to stop you from completing the ceremony."[6]

Betonie's realization is cryptic, indirect. Yet Tayo himself realizes the truth of the old man's words: "His sickness was only part of something larger, and his cure would be found only in something great and inclusive of everything."[7] Betonie finally gives the malaise a name: witchery. All of his other problems, the ones with which the novel leads off, are a part of this larger thing, named only here, halfway through the story. After Betonie has voiced the central concerns of the book, Tayo is charged with living them out. He descends back into the moving world and is immediately tempted by the witchery to "sin" against the ceremonies that become Indian-speak for moral choices. He succumbs and accepts a ride from his friend Harley. Tayo gets drunk and is in danger of falling from his path to recovery. In what becomes a symbol for spiritual malaise, Tayo vomits, "trying to vomit out everything—all the past, all his life."[8] He has hit the bottom but he is finally in motion, steps backward notwithstanding. After his first temptation, Tayo heads into the mountains to retrieve his uncle's wayward cattle. It is here, like in most fairy tales, that he has his third encounter, his third chance to get it right.

The third source of Tayo's healing, and the most significant and lasting, is the mysterious woman named Ts'eh. Tayo has gone into the mountains on a mission to retrieve his uncle's cattle in an episode that can only be described as half western and half vision quest. Along the way he meets Ts'eh. From the first her portrait is lovingly and completely drawn. We have no idea what Ku'oosh looks like and Betonie is given the barest physical outline. Ts'eh, on the other hand, is lavished with description in inverse proportion to how much she speaks:

> She was wearing a man's shirt tucked into a yellow skirt that hung below her knees. Pale buckskin moccasins reached the edge of her skirt. The silver buttons up the side of each moccasin had rainbirds carved on them. She wasn't much older than he was, but she wore her hair long, like the old women did, pinned back in a knot.[9]

Ts'eh, who has appeared, as if from nowhere, remains mysterious. She allows him to water his horse by saying, "'Help yourself,'" and then invites him inside her house by saying, "'Come inside,'" and then, after Tayo follows her inside, she tells him: "'Sit down. Eat.'" And as he eats stew she makes what is for her small talk: "'The sky is clear. You can see the stars tonight.'"[10] And then, just as suddenly as she appears, she and Tayo have sex:

> He watched her face, and her eyes never shifted; they were with him while she moved out of her clothes and while she slipped his jeans down his legs, stroking his thighs. She unbuttoned his shirt, and all he was aware of was the heat of his own breathing and the warmth radiating from his belly, pulsing between his legs. He was afraid of being lost, so

he repeated trail marks to himself: this is my mouth tasting the salt of her brown breasts; this is my voice calling out to her. He eased himself deeper within her and felt the warmth close around him like river sand, softly giving way under foot, then closing firmly around the ankle in cloudy warm water. But he did not get lost, and he smiled at her as she held his hips and pulled him closer. He let the motion carry him, and he could feel the momentum within, at first almost imperceptible, gathering in his belly. When it came, it was the edge of a steep riverbank crumbling under the downpour until suddenly it all broke loose and collapsed into itself.[11]

The next morning, at dawn, Tayo feels compelled to sing the sunrise chant of his people. (After sex like that who wouldn't want to sing?) For her part, Ts'eh remains silent. She fixes Tayo breakfast and while he eats, she busies herself with a ceremony of sorts—combining cloth, earth, tobacco, and plants. She says nothing when Tayo leaves the house. All in all, she seems like the dream woman she is—she provides food and sex and gentle direction in life without burdening her man with unnecessary conversation, much less with her needs.

Tayo finds his uncle's cattle and then heads down the mountain. When Tayo returns a few weeks later the cabin is empty. She is gone. Nonetheless, just as he entered her, she has entered him. When Tayo dreams now, his dreams are as peaceful as erotic dreams can be.

> He dreamed with her, dreams that lasted
> all night, dreams full of warm deep caressing
> and lingering desire which left him sleeping
> peacefully until dawn (. . .)
> He was overwhelmed by the love he felt
> for her; tears filled his eyes and the ache in his
> throat ran deep into his chest.[12]

It is this love that finally cracks open Tayo's heart like a window propped open with a shoe. He realizes "He had lost nothing. . . . Josiah and Rocky were not far away. They were close; they had always been close."[13] With the burgeoning of his personal love comes a corresponding rebirth of the land. The drought, for which Tayo has always felt responsible, has broken. The rain has replenished the land—plants, flowers, insects—all have come alive. The links between Tayo's healing at the hands and between the legs of Ts'eh and the regrowth of the drought-stricken land are highlighted when Tayo sees Ts'eh again.

The tenor of their relationship has changed, or if the relationship itself hasn't changed, its literary representation has. Gone is the speechlessness of sex, the focus on bodies and desire. This is replaced with an almost saintly nimbus that surrounds Ts'eh as she gathers medicines from the land. We are given no further descriptions of their lovemaking. [To do so would be merely pornographic—just as in most movies we see sex between characters who want each other or who might lose each other but never between characters who already peacefully possess each other. The sex in *Ceremony* and in the cinema is desperate, never uxoric.] Tayo is finally at peace in the dreamland of his love for her and her love for him.

But the logic of Tayo's troubles and of his healing demands that his journey can't end here. He is not the only one who is sick—the sickness, we have been reminded often, is not limited to him alone; the people, the land, the entire world is sick—and so his cure cannot be found by himself. He must reconcile himself with his community and confront the problems there as well as within himself.

To reenter the world means that he must leave his mountain woman. All of their time together is marked by a tender terror at the temporality of their uxorious paradise. They collect herbs together and rebuild a shrine. Ts'eh is as distraught as Tayo. Toward the very end he sees that Ts'eh is crying. He asks her why she is so upset. "'The end of the story. They want to change it. They want it to end here, the way all their stories end, encircling slowly to choke the life away.'"[14] She continues with ominous words of warning: "'They'll call to you. Friendly voices. If you come quietly, they will take you and lock you in the white walls of the hospital. But if you don't go with them, they'll hunt you down, and take you any way they can. Because it is the only ending they understand.'"[15] In the end she will not fight at his side. She appears, like some tutelary spirit, at times of need, bearing advice, but Tayo must deal with his problems on his own.

NATIVE AMERICAN FICTION: A USER'S MANUAL

Now all the pieces of the book come together in rapid fire. The root of all the witchery, the great transformative act, is revealed as the explosion of the world's first nuclear bomb at White Sands, and the open uranium mine near Laguna is where the final confrontation between Tayo and his friends, between healing and witchery, takes place. Only now does Tayo recognize the full extent of the evil that surrounds him:

> There was no end to it; it knew no boundaries; and he had arrived at the point of convergence where the fate of all living things, and even the earth, had been laid. From the jungles of his dreaming he recognized why the Japanese voices had merged with Laguna voices, with Josiah's voice and Rocky's voice; the lines of cultures and worlds were drawn in flat dark lines on fine light sand, converging in the middle of witchery's final ceremonial sand painting. From that time on, human beings were one clan again, united by the fate the destroyers planned for all of them, for all living things . . ."[16]

Shortly after this realization Tayo's "friends"—Emo and Harley and Pinkie who are really only the agents of witchery—come after him and he escapes into the hills. Deprived of Tayo as the sacrificial victim, they turn on Harley and torture him in the abandoned uranium mine—stringing him up in a barbed-wire fence, cutting off the pads of his hands, fingers, feet,

THE MYTH OF MYTH

and toes. This forces Tayo into his final confrontation with the witchery and with himself. He is tempted to stab Emo in the head with a screwdriver, but he holds himself back. He realizes this is what the witchery wants. "The witchery had almost ended the story according to its plan. . . . Their deadly ritual for the autumn solstice [sic] would have been completed by him."[17]

As it is, Tayo had enough strength from his healing—a path set out for him by Betonie, guided by Ts'eh, and finished by him alone—to do the right thing. And with a sigh of relief, Tayo's precarious world rights itself. The past comes into delicious concord with the present. The world is at peace.

Textual Healing

The differences between *Ceremony* and *Love Medicine* are obvious. Erdrich's efforts and moves are most interesting when viewed up close. Her syntax, the structure of her sentences, is what enables her to motivate the physical symbols that give the book meaning. She is able to maneuver her words in such a way as to animate cars and pies and baby jumpers and turkey hearts. Silko, on the other hand, seems less interested in the sentence as an aesthetic unit. More broadly, there is very little use of symbolism. In one of the earliest sections quoted in this essay, taken from the beginning of the novel Silko describes Tayo's troubles:

the coiled springs kept squeaking even after
he lay still again, calling up humid dreams of

black night and loud voices rolling him over
and over again like debris caught in a flood.
Tonight the singing had come first, squeaking
out of the iron bed, a man singing in Spanish,
the melody of a familiar love song, two words
again and again . . .[18]

In this passage and throughout the novel Silko
favors simile over metaphor and ritual over symbol.
The "coiled springs" are what call up the dreams Tayo
suffers from. The loud voices he hears are described
as being "like debris caught in a flood." Silko's figurative language works by leading back to the central
element or landscape that defines her scenes—in this
case, the presence of water. These images or elements
don't symbolize anything. They just flavor Tayo's emotions, heightening an already plainly stated confusion,
weakness, or powerlessness. The very appropriateness
of her images, thus contained in simile, renders them
unable to lift the novel out of a realist or physicalist
mode of representation, and the images smack more
clearly of the early Romantics than they do of the
Symbolists. The perfect concord between Tayo's emotions and the landscape or environment in which he
exists can be traced back to the early eighteenth century. In Chateaubriand's *Atala,* for example, when the
two main characters consummate their love, nature
cooperates:

We were listening to the roar of the storm,
when suddenly I felt a tear fall on my
breast. (. . .)

At these words a cry escaped me which rang through the solitude, and my ecstatic outbursts mingled with the din of the storm. (. . .)

Atala could offer only feeble resistance, and the ecstatic moment had come, when suddenly an impetuous bolt of lightning, followed by a clap of thunder, furrowed the thickness of the shadows, filled the forest with fire and brimstone, and split a tree apart at our very feet.[19]

There are differences between Chateaubriand and Silko—the atmospherics in *Atala* partially obscure the consummation of desire and stand in for it (not unlike the train going into the tunnel during *North by Northwest*), whereas in Silko, the emotions are not extended by metaphor so much as they are linked—human emotions are the cause of atmospheric disturbance. Silko's world is, ironically, far more anthropocentric than Chateaubriand's.

In comparison, Erdrich's symbols work because of the very distance they first seem to have from what they symbolize—something that is also done very well and quite originally in Toni Morrison's writing. Erdrich and Morrison create strange pairs—objects such as dimes or parrots or pies or cars matched with unlikely or unexpected emotions. Silko's magic comes from an entirely different source. Instead of symbol she is interested in ritual.

Tayo's actions are not symbolic, they are real. When he needs healing it is because he is sick. His

NATIVE AMERICAN FICTION: A USER'S MANUAL

healing ceremonies, unlike the turkey hearts in *Love Medicine,* do not stand in or represent anything else. Instead of objects such as turkey hearts or cars, we have physical action, sometimes repetitive physical action. These actions—going to Betonie and then back to the sheep camp, riding the mule with Harley and riding around in pickup trucks with Harley, Emo, and Pinkie, going to retrieve the horses, walking off the mountain, sleeping with Ts'eh—are what carry the weight of meaning for the book and seem to be related to the myths of purification that are sliced up and scattered throughout the book.

The Myth of Myth

These purification myths are central to how *Ceremony* has been framed and have come to be considered central to the Native American texts in general. The use of myth has become one of the defining attributes of the genre.

There are a number of myths, ostensibly Pueblo myths (though there are some that are "new," obviously invented by Silko) broadcast like seeds throughout the text. Some of them are short, others are quite long. The most important and longest myth included in the text is a drought myth.

The action of this myth is simple: at some ancient time a man/spirit arrives and asks the people if they want to learn some magic. The villagers can't resist and so say yes. He impresses them and they become so entranced that they neglect their duties and responsibilities. For this the people are punished:

Our mother
Nau'ts'ity'i
was very angry
over this
over the way
all of them
even Ma'see'wi and Ou'yu'ye'wi
fooled around with this
magic.

"I've had enough of that,"
she said,
"If they like that magic so much
let them live off it."

So she took
the plants and grass from them.
No baby animals were born.
She took the
rainclouds with her.[20]

The myth quest is simple: the characters have to find a way to heal their world. The two characters who carry this load are Hummingbird and Fly. They go underground to the fourth world and ask Mother what to do. First they have to purify their town, and they need old Buzzard to do this. When they find Buzzard he tells them they need tobacco. Down again they go to the fourth world, and they are told to ask Caterpillar. They visit him and get tobacco from him. From there they go back to old Buzzard who receives the tobacco and purifies the town. Mother then agrees, finally, to return the rainclouds:

> The storm clouds returned
> the grass and plants started growing again.
>
> . . . .
> So she told them
> "Stay out of trouble
> from now on.
>
> It isn't very easy
> to fix up things again.
> Remember that
> next time
> some ck'o'yo magician
> comes to town."[21]

The myth is a cautionary tale—mind your manners, do as you're told, be responsible, or bad things will happen. The myth seems to mirror the larger movements of the novel. We have an all-pervasive sickness, a drought that affects all the people, and then gradual steps—back and forth—are taken toward healing and a cure, which is finally achieved at the end. But this is where the similarities between myth and book end.

For instance, while both Tayo and Hummingbird/Fly have what are in effect "stopping places" on their respective quests, the *quality* of their actions is different. There are major differences in why, how, and where they stop. Moreover, in the myth, Hummingbird and Fly don't feel or think or react or struggle. For them it's just one thing and then another, first to the Mother, then to old Buzzard, and then to the Mother again, from there to Caterpillar and back to Buzzard. The myth, like many myths, functions only on one level, in one register with very little of the heightening, shading, and blending that is present in modern prose.

In terms of style, the myths are paratactical to the extreme. "The storm clouds returned/the grass and plants started growing again./There was food/and the people were happy again."[22] There are virtually no subordinate clauses in this myth-passage or any others. The prose, on the other hand, only functions because of subordination:

> *During that last summer* they had ridden across these flats to round up the speckled cattle and brand the calves. He took the pickup across the dip slowly, *almost tenderly, as if the old truck were the blind white mule, too old to be treated roughly any more.* He was thinking about Harley and Leroy; *about Helen Jean and himself.* How much longer would they last? How long before one of them got stabbed in a bar fight, *not just knocked out?* How long before this old truck swerved off the road *or head-on into a bus? But it didn't make much difference anyway.* (italics mine)[23]

In this paragraph, more or less taken at random, hypotactic constructions make up over a third of the

NATIVE AMERICAN FICTION: A USER'S MANUAL

text. Silko hangs her descriptions off her main clauses and never obscures the central thrust of her sentences or her paragraphs. By careful subordination Silko creates both the momentum and the images that propel her narrative forward. The myth, stylistically speaking, does not have this kind of drive.

Moreover, the meaning and sense freighted in these two different modes also couldn't be more different. The myth is actual . . . it doesn't mean anything beyond its subject. When Hummingbird and Fly go down to the fourth world, they are not metaphorically flying down there, they are actually flying down there, and their flight does not *signify* anything. So, when the myth-narrative shifts directions or a new episode begins, it is only the "next step" in a sequence of steps; there is nothing to *cause* the next step except the advice of benign and seemingly omniscient characters. This kind of travel—without a thought in the world as to the significance or deeper meaning, without the presence of a single metaphor, simile, zeugma, or rambling comparison—brings with it a kind of innocence. A tribal naïveté that has been the stock and trade of literary representations of Indian myths from the eighteenth century onward.

The prose in *Ceremony,* however, is very different from the staged innocence of myth. Tayo's "turns," the points at which the narrative shifts direction or lunges forward, all focus on healing. There are three attempts—once with Ku'osh, Betonie, and Ts'eh—and at each turn, Tayo and his quest change. But unlike the drought myth that paces the prose, Tayo's turns are psychological not atavistic, and—even though they

THE MYTH OF MYTH

look nativistically ritualistic—they have therapeutic and literary ancestors, not Indian ancestors.

For instance, when Ku'osh (a passive healer) is unable to provide a cure for Tayo, Tayo goes to Betonie's where he is set on his path, ostensibly as the result of powerful syncretic magic. Here is the beginning of his healing:

> "My uncle Josiah was there that day. Yet I knew he couldn't have been there. He was thousands of miles away, at home in Laguna. We were in the Philippine jungles. I understand that. I know he couldn't have been there. But I've got this feeling and it won't go away even though I know he wasn't there. I feel like he was there. I feel like he was there with those Japanese soldiers who died." Tayo's voice was shaking; he could feel the tears pushing into his eyes. Suddenly the feeling was there, as strong as it had been that day in the jungle. "He loved me. He loved me, and I didn't do anything to save him."
> "When did he die?"
> "While we were gone. He died because there was no one to help him search for the cattle after they were stolen."
> "Rocky," Betonie said softly, "tell me about Rocky."[24]

And it is precisely at that point that the true active ingredient in the narrative becomes obvious: Tayo is going through the "talking cure" and dredging up

NATIVE AMERICAN FICTION: A USER'S MANUAL

perfect traumas with which the modern reader will be very familiar—guilt, responsibility, and the terrors of choice. Tayo's healing is Freudian even if it is given a Native sheen when he and Betonie ride into the hills and make white corn sand paintings. This is not to belittle the pageant of ceremonial healing, which, visually at least, moves the story along, but it is important to recognize that this second "turn" in the novel has its roots in, and gleans its sense from psychoanalysis and psychotherapy. They are what inform the beginning of Tayo's cure—his first steps are the steps toward articulating his problems, and then he sets out to make them right by first recovering his uncle's cattle.

Tayo's second cure, literally at the hands of Ts'eh, deviates from the path of psychoanalysis, and while it seems to nestle closer to the earth and the mythic type of Ts'eh, it actually springs from different soil altogether. It is ironic that in a novel praised for its feminist outlook and sensibility the central male character is "healed" through intercourse. The women in *Ceremony*—most importantly Ts'eh and Night Swan— are earth mothers whose function it is to center and educate their men, they have no reality of their own. And while Ts'eh, it is suggested, is the physically carnate version of a character from a Pueblo myth, she hails from the pages of literature not from the Pueblos. In much of Western literature women exist to educate men and this phenomenon has been well explored in critical work. The worst example of this in literature about Indians is the Sioux woman in Larry Watson's *Montana 1948*. It feels as though her only purpose in the novel is to be raped so that the white characters can learn from her trauma. She has no reality of her own and is nothing more than a two-dimensional stockpile of what Watson thought of as the most abject and vulnerable qualities a character could have: female, Indian, poor, and indentured. One could argue that *Ceremony* is "feminist" because it contains strong women, but Delilah and Eve were strong, too . . .

The real source of Tayo's sexual healing with Ts'eh has a not-so-remote ancestor in Hemingway, not in Pueblo myth. Compare Tayo's experience, which we have seen before in this essay

> He watched her face, and her eyes never shifted; they were with him while she moved out of her clothes and while she slipped his jeans down his legs, stroking his thighs. She unbuttoned his shirt, and all he was aware of was the heat of his own breathing and the warmth radiating from his belly, pulsing between his legs. . . . He let the motion carry him, and he could feel the momentum within, at first almost imperceptible, gathering in his belly. When it came, it was the edge of a steep riverbank crumbling under the downpour until suddenly it all broke loose and collapsed into itself.[25]

with Nick Adams's experience in "Fathers and Sons":

> Could you say that she did first what no one has ever done better and mention plump

brown legs, flat belly, hard little breasts, well
holding arms, quick searching tongue, the
flat eyes, the good taste of mouth, then un-
comfortably, tightly, sweetly, moistly, lovely,
tightly, achingly, fully, finally, unendingly,
never-endingly, never-to-endingly, suddenly
ended, the great bird flown like an owl in the
twilight . . .[26]

The episode is about Nick Adams's first sexual encounter with the Ojibwe girl Trudy. It is from her and
with her that he learns about sex. She barely speaks,
just like Ts'eh. She is blithely open to having sex, just
like Ts'eh. There is no sense, in either case, that there
is a sexual exchange, equal or otherwise. The erotic
eye is only focused on the men. Both passages end
with a focus on the man's orgasm and never bother
to contemplate even the possibility of female pleasure. And more than focusing on the man's pleasure,
each passage begins with daringly direct physical
descriptions—belly, breasts, legs—and the closer the
man gets to orgasm, the more tenuous ties the prose
has to the action until, just when the man lifts off, so
does the prose—aloft on the wings of metaphor, on
the crumbling riverbank and the great bird flown at
night.

Both passages are beautiful. Both are well constructed and heart quickening. And clearly, Tayo's
sexual healing does not parallel the myths in *Ceremony* as much as it parallels Nick Adams's sexual
education. Or, it does parallel a myth, just not the
one presented to us by Silko. The foundational myth

it relies on is the myth of the educationally available Indian woman, whose true ancestors can be found in the experienced and knowing educators in Greek pastoral novels such as *Daphnis and Chloe* or the *Ethiopica*. In these early romances there were usually two innocent main characters who were trying, as best as they could, to lose that innocence. The genre demanded that the girl remain a virgin while the boy-hero needed to know more, but only a bit more. Longus and the other writers of these romances evolved the "educational stranger"—an older, more experienced woman the boy-hero could not possibly love, but who could teach the mysteries of sex, as education for his future possession of his beloved. In *Ceremony* we do not have a love interest like Chloe, but we do have the sexually available and more experienced Ts'eh who educates him.

~

Another big difference between the prose and the Pueblo myth—in addition to Tayo's "talking cure" and his sexual healing—is how, after each healing turn in *Ceremony,* Tayo's faith is tested. After he leaves Betonie, Tayo meets Harley and Leroy. These two will appear again and again and threaten to pull Tayo off his proper path. Betonie has even warned him this would happen. "'This has been going on for a long long time now. [he told Tayo] It's up to you. Don't let them stop you. Don't let them finish off this world.'"[27]

But the pleasures of oblivion are tempting, no matter how good it feels to heal. As Tayo rides in the pickup truck with Harley and Leroy and Helen

Jean, he resists as long as he can, until he can't take it anymore.

> "We'll give you a cure! We know how,
> don't we?" Harley was bouncing on the seat,
> and he made the whole truck sway on its weak
> springs. Helen Jean squealed, and the bottle of
> wine she was holding splashed all over them.
> Tayo grabbed it and swallowed what was left
> in the bottle.[28]

Toward the very end of the book when he sees Ts'eh for the last time she warns him (just as Betonie warned him earlier) that "they" will try and stop him, that the witchery will try and beat him. And sure enough, shortly after leaving Ts'eh he meets Harley and Leroy again. Once again they ride around in the truck, and once again Tayo is tempted to give up his quest for healing.

There is one final test of Tayo's resolve, one final temptation that is whispered into his ear. This time he must draw on his own resolve, see things as they are without Betonie or Ts'eh's prodding, as if taking his first few baby steps on his own. When Harley is being tortured, Tayo has the urge to kill Emo with a screwdriver: "He visualized the contours of Emo's skull; the GI haircut exposed thin bone at the temples, bone that would flex slightly before it gave way under the thrust of the steel edge."[29] But, in the end, Tayo resists and wins the battle against witchery by saying "no" to violence and "yes" to being Indian and embracing peace.

All of these tests—the step toward healing and the challenge to his conviction and faith—are not represented in any of the myths that Silko uses in *Ceremony*. In those myths there is no "inner struggle" or questing for the "right decision." The drought myths and the myths of transformation in *Ceremony* involve simple cause and effect, action and reaction—there is no sense of emotional struggle or self-doubt. Tayo's struggles have more to do with the temptations of Christ in the desert than with Pueblo myth.

> Then Jesus was led up by the Spirit into the wilderness to be tempted by the devil. . . .
> And the tempter came and said to him, "If you are the Son of God, command these stones to become loaves of bread." (. . .)
> Then the devil took him to the holy city, and set him on the pinnacle of the temple, and said to him, "If you are the Son of God, throw yourself down; for it is written,
> 'He will give his angels charge of you,'" (. . .)
> Again, the devil took him to a very high mountain, and showed him all the kingdoms of the world and the glory of them; and he said to him, "All these I will give you, if you will fall down and worship me." Then Jesus said to him, "Begone, Satan! for it is written,
> 'You shall worship the Lord your God and him only shall you serve.'"
> Then the devil left him, and behold, angels came and ministered to him.[30]

The similarities are striking. In each case there are the multiple and serial temptations that are savored and then rejected; the same extreme landscapes (deserts and mountains) with the ultimate moments occurring on mountaintops; and the same strength of character that develops as a result of temptation.

A less extreme example of the tensions between proper behavior, the proper path, and temptation, sin, and inappropriate behavior can be found in literature. Milton argued in his *Areopagitica* that good and evil were necessarily intertwined and that untested faith is not real faith. It is necessary to put yourself into contact with sin in order to have the opportunity to reject it. He writes:

> I cannot praise a fugitive and cloistered virtue, unexercised and unbreathed, that never sallies out and sees her adversary but slinks out of the race, where that immortal garland is to be run for, not without dust and heat. Assuredly we bring not innocence into the world, we bring impurity much rather; that which purifies us is trial, and trial is by what is contrary.[31]

The question of interpretation is a pesky one in general, and even peskier when we are confronted with material that looks different and seems different than that found in "mainstream" or "Western" literature. The mythic material in *Ceremony,* even the book itself, seems to come from some other place.

But *Ceremony* hails from much closer to home (our shared modern home, that is) than we could have imagined. It is no accident that Tayo's moral and sociopolitical predicaments mirror Luke Skywalker's. He, like Skywalker, is an orphan of sorts, raised by his extended family. Like Skywalker, Tayo must chose between the good and the bad and is tempted up until the very end to go over to the dark side of the force. Like Skywalker his home is a very dry environment and both Luke and Tayo have their biggest moments of self-doubt in appropriately wet and humid environments. It is also no accident that both *Star Wars* and *Ceremony* came out in 1977. Even if all of that is coincidental, it is not accidental. Both stories are products of their time and the stories that surround them. It should be clear by now that the novel turns on psychological investigation, layered meaning and significance, and that it takes up many of the issues that are the stock and trade of the novel, not of the culture. Silko, however, sees her writing as Pueblo writing. Not just Native in spirit, but Native in fact:

> Where I come from the words most highly
> valued are those spoken from the heart,
> unpremeditated and unrehearsed. . . . But
> the particular language being spoken isn't as
> important as what a speaker is trying to say,
> and this emphasis on the story itself stems,
> I believe, from a view of narrative particular
> to the Pueblo and other Native American
> peoples—that is, that language *is* story.[32]

NATIVE AMERICAN FICTION: A USER'S MANUAL

Silko goes on to claim that "many individual words have their own stories" and that this "perspective on narrative—of story within story, the idea that one story is only the beginning of many stories and the sense that stories never truly end—represents an important contribution of Native American cultures to the English language."[33]

That words have "stories" inside of them is very well known. It is called etymology. That there are stories within stories was well established in Homer's time and is a sentiment and a technique that has been used productively in so many traditions as to be universal.

One has to ask, if "language *is* story," and if the Pueblo view of storytelling is not to "fragment stories of experience," why does myth in *Ceremony* get chopped up and spread out to compost throughout the book? And, if heart-speak matters more than language or form, then why position myth in the book to make it look like poetry? For example:

> Thought-Woman, the spider,
> named things and
> as she named them
> they appeared.[34]

The impetus behind this phenomenon is that something is gained by looking like poetry, even though the myth is *not* poetry. "It is," says John Hollander,

> common and convenient for most people who don't read carefully to use "poetry" to mean

"writing in some kind of verse," and to regard thereby the design without considering the materials. The most popular verse form in America today—the ubiquitous jingle readers identify with "poetry" even as, fifty or sixty years ago, they did anything that rhymed—is

> a kind of free verse
> without any special
> constraints on it except
> those imposed by
> the notion—also
> generally accepted—that
> the strip the lines
> make as they run
> down the page (the
> familiar strip with the
> jagged
> right-hand edge) not
> be too wide[35]

Anything can be scrunched onto the left margin or centered on the page, but that doesn't make it poetry. Myth can be set the same way, but that doesn't make it poetic. In any event, the "mythic mode" never lasts very long—three or four pages at most in *Ceremony*—and the "myth" is literal. When Silko writes that Hummingbird and Fly took pollen and prayer sticks and went to see Buzzard, they, the Hummingbird and the Fly, did exactly that. When they go down to the fourth world, they are literally going there. Myth is literal, not metaphorical. Metaphor is a situation in which one thing is used to designate another. In many Native American myths, certainly in the ones Silko uses, this is not the case. The action and environment described within the myths are resolutely literal. Most Native American "myths" function this way, which is why they are not poetry. When most people describe myths as poetic, and when they arrange myth to appear like verse, what they are trying to convey is that the myth is beautiful or meaningful. They mean that myth is significant. And even if the myth is beautiful or meaningful, that does not turn it into poetry. Poetry, to dip into Hollander again, makes use of the same elements as fiction—"fable, 'image,' metaphor—all the material of the nonliteral."[36] That doesn't even begin to completely define what fiction or poetry is, but it's a start. And the reason we only get snippets of "myth" is that as writers and readers we are conditioned to want and expect novels to function on a different level. We know that in novels *what* a character says or does to another character, and *how* it is written, means more than what is physically happening on the page. When Tayo refrains from killing Emo, he has achieved a victory greater than simply refusing to be a murderer.

In Silko, the presence of myth, set apart from the prose, outside the action, in small doses, ultimately contradicts the claim for "mythic" or "culturally derived storytelling." So, what is it doing there? Myth is set up to look like verse or epigraph and is intended to suggest that the precepts found there are deep, extra-specially meaningful, important, and outside of and different from the novel form being used by the authors. Myth and language here are not important in and of themselves. They are important because they lend resonance or deeper sonority to the action of the novel. Tribal myth, devoid of context and continuity, serves only to thicken the prose-stew, like the flour my mother adds to her delicious gravy; it has to do with consistency, not taste.

And the sentiment in *Ceremony* that story is ceremony, that stories are alive, while it might have something to do with Pueblo philosophy, is not unique. To return to Milton, he writes that "books are not absolutely dead things, but do contain a potency of life in them to be as active as that soul was whose progeny they are; nay, they do preserve as in a vial the purest efficacy and extraction of that living intellect that bred them."[37]

This is especially true of *Ceremony* and its creator, Silko. The novel is an extraction of Silko's living intellect—an intellect and sensibility that are beholden to much more than she and her critics give her credit for. To see *Ceremony* as the modern embodiment of ancient myth or as echoing on another register the same truths that the myths in novels have been speaking for centuries is to mistake how the book looks for what it does. The myths are, ironically, much more visual than actual. That they look like myths as they've been presented in text by folklorists and anthropologists for the last eighty years is more significant than what the myths might mean to Pueblo people.

This is not to say that the myths that Silko includes in *Ceremony* are superfluous or that they are somehow inauthentic. Again, to focus on authenticity is to ob-

NATIVE AMERICAN FICTION: A USER'S MANUAL

scure true vision. Beyond plot there is no similarity between the myth and the prose. There is a relationship between the two, but it is their differences that are significant, not their superficial similarities. We shouldn't interpret the book as myth or as Pueblo storytelling; we can't honestly see the book through the myth, the book is not Pueblo myth even though (and partly because) it contains it. To try and read the book through culture or as culture is to miss the chance to interpret and understand what is wonderful and vital about the novel. To assume the myths are important because they are Pueblo or because they seem authentic or because we've been told they are, is also to miss the point.

It is the very incommensurability of the mythic forms used by Silko and the novel form in which they are couched that is interesting. It is not a problem that the myths and the prose, the quests represented in the myths and Tayo's quest, do not work in the same way or in any way that is remotely similar. It is their difference and the tension created by their difference that is wonderful. If Milton is right, and trial occurs by what is contrary, then Silko's novel progresses by virtue of struggle: a struggle between the myth and the prose.

It is important to remember that struggle itself is, after all, only a comparison with an outcome, if not a winner. And this is exactly what Silko has done, and done brilliantly. She has, in Proust's words, done what artists and truthseekers do: the artist "takes two different things, establishes the relationship between them, and imprisons them within the necessary construction of a beautiful style."[38]

THE MYTH OF MYTH

Many, if not all, novels share this quality in one way or another. And there are many different ways it can take shape. Within the story: where the characters are and where they have been; where they are and where they are going; the character's self-impression and the impression others make of him; the emotional climate before momentous action and the climate afterwards. In *Burning Down the House,* novelist Charles Baxter makes an excellent point when he says that this comparative impulse common to stories or novels is also common in ourselves—we begin to draft the story of our own life by comparing it to the lives of those around us.[39] The internal differences between the myth and the prose should by now be fairly obvious. But if we take a step back from the text, the differences become even more glaring. Silko has made the distance between these myths and the prose visual, not just textual. The myth is centered on the page and dressed up as free verse when there is no compelling reason having to do with the content or tradition of the myth to make it necessary to do so.

So what, then, is the relationship between the myth and the novel? The relationship is, aside from very thin and superficial "quests" that take place in both, the very distance between them—it is the distance between the worlds contained in each that matters. Tayo's world is rife with forces—some evil, some good—all of them crossed and twined and writhing through the walls of that reality. Tayo's is a complicated world that is thick with emotion and effort and a palpable and painful human straining. The world of the myths, on the other hand, is a blissful almost emotionless nirvana. There are problems in the myth-reality that Hummingbird and Fly try to fix, mistakes are made in the myth-reality. Even so, life in the myth is astonishingly free of tension or anxiety. In the myth-reality, pain itself is quiet and matter-of-fact. There is no confusion here. No doubt. It is a decidedly un-novelistic reality. In terms of action and in terms of language, the myth-reality is the only quiet place in the novel. And it is exactly that kind of peace that Tayo is so intent on finding. The novel is always wistfully looking over its shoulder at this myth-reality. Myth here functions as a kind of cultural nostalgia. It is, in contrast to Tayo's adult life, the uncomplicated childhood of Indian culture, and Tayo's inner child, as well as the reader's inner Indian, who yearn for it. Nick Adams could have been talking about just this kind of nostalgia for the never-land of Indian life when he reflects on his first sexual awakening with the hapless Trudy: "Long time ago good. Now no good."[40]

~

And there is really no escaping this kind of distinction if we persist in interpreting *Ceremony* on the basis of Pueblo storytelling or Pueblo myth. The problem—and this extends to most other Native American novels—with interpreting *Ceremony* is one of orientation: it is fruitless to ask questions about where the book is coming from. It is much more interesting to look at where it is going and how the reader is being carried along. To ask questions about the book's origins or about what it represents—Indian perspective, tribal myth, etcetera—is necessarily to get involved with questions of authenticity. To ask questions about the authenticity of *Ceremony* or *Love Medicine* or *Fools Crow* is to rob the books of their status as literature. It doesn't really matter whether or not the myths Silko uses in *Ceremony* are Pueblo or if they are accurate or if she grew up hearing them. I should stress that it doesn't matter to anyone and should not matter to anyone except the Pueblo people themselves. It doesn't matter because the relevance of the myths is determined by their relationship to the book itself. The myths we read belong to the book, not vice versa. Why they matter is no longer a cultural question because the sense of the myths is activated and employed by the plot and prose around them.

If we can manage to tear our gaze away from the crib and cradle of "pure" or "authentic" culture and redirect it at the more interesting and active adolescence of the prose, we will be able to do better than Tayo. We won't just remember the story, we will also understand how it works.

The Spirit Lives On

In the fall of 2000 the Weisman Art Museum on the banks of the Mississippi River mounted a strange exhibit: a collection of Native American art produced by Minnesota Native artists. The paintings themselves were a study in the multiform aspects of technique, subject, and theme that is common to Native art nationwide. Most of the pieces were amazing, were wonderful. What was strange was the accompanying title and text for the exhibit: "Listening With The Heart."

After coming in the main entrance and taking a left into the gallery space, past a few Warhols and other pieces of contemporary art, the visitor was greeted by a large plaque that attempted to explain the philosophy of the exhibit. It began by stating that the "experience of listening with the heart cannot be captured in words." And then, after stating (with words) the uselessness of words, it read:

> The heart cannot be convinced by words alone; the heart must understand. Words can explain the work, but experience can tell us only how the work is similar to, different

from, typical of. . . . Experience leaves the
work mute. Understanding gained through
listening with the heart allows the art to speak
to us.

Never mind that the writer confused his own concept of "experience" with his attack on the "word."
That is, first we are told that words are not sufficient
for a true experience of the exhibit (which the curious viewer has yet to see), rather, the "heart must understand," and in the next sentence experience itself
(the only true way any heart can become wiser, one
would think) comes under direct fire because all it
can do is help us refer to things we have already seen.
I don't think that experience leaves us as mute as this
perplexing plaque does. As if this weren't mystical
enough, the text goes on to say:

the work in this exhibit invites us into a
conversation—a heart to heart talk in which
we can listen to these artists as they describe,
through their art, a reality in which the human,
natural, and spiritual worlds are not separate
distinct categories but a continuum.

By now the viewer (this viewer anyway) was totally
confused. Even though words and experience—the
only two ways human beings come to an understanding of anything—fall short of the mark, we will nonetheless have a "heart to heart talk."

Then to the paintings. And the exhibit became
really strange. The paintings, by established artists

NATIVE AMERICAN FICTION: A USER'S MANUAL

such as George Morrison, Frank Big Bear, Jr., and Norval Morrisseau, were stunning in range and technique. Other lesser known artists such as Julie Buffalohead and Jim Denomie explored fantastic and daring thematic terrain—from popular conceptions of Indianness to wry commentary on Indian gaming, colonialism, to non-self-pitying looks at social trauma and modern Indian life. Denomie favors "crude" landscapes—mesas and mountains tacked to the canvas—around which hover armored cars being chased by Indians on horses that could fly. These landscapes, because of their mixing of caricatured icon and earthy color, possess a startling ability to communicate the complexities of modern life. Buffalohead's work was more concerned with texture, and her technique was impressive: the depth of her scenes and their ambiguous subjects combined to create haunting and accomplished visions.

I don't think I have ever seen an exhibit that was more conceptually complex, thematically nuanced, and intellectually demanding. As a whole, it addressed the run of Indian life from the crushing power of historical and folkloric stereotype to the future of Indian gaming. The paintings invited the viewer to enter an intellectual playing field of metaphor, image, and theme; it was as if the exhibit was a carnival fun house that, instead of bending the viewer, bent the view. The viewers' expectations and understandings of Indian history and thought were challenged and transformed. Sadly, this was all lost on the person or people who wrote the accompanying text. It is sometimes difficult to say exactly what a piece of art is "trying to do," but what was absolutely clear about the exhibit was that it was resolutely and defiantly nonemotional and nonmystical. There were, to be sure, artists like Patrick DesJarlait who took their inspiration from life scenes and from the culture. But the closest any of the paintings came to replicating or continuing the spiritual and cultural stereotyping that strangles Indian art was Morriseau's sequence of a "Man Changing into a Thunderbird." Even these paintings, however, used culture as a way to ponder the issue of transformation—a theme present in art and writing from antiquity onward.

As a viewer, sorting out the paintings and the significance was a challenging intellectual endeavor, so why did the text plastered all over the exhibit make such strong claims on our hearts and emotions? Why were we encouraged to interpret the paintings with everything except our intellects? Why is there such a strain and stain of anti-intellectualism in Native American art, not to mention Native literary criticism?

The problem was not unlike the one faced by Toni Morrison upon the publication of her novel, *Jazz*. Some journalist at the *New York Times* who *should* have known better summed up *Jazz* as being soulful and brilliant and finished with this flourish: "*Jazz*— you just have to feel it." The reviewer couldn't have been more wrong. Jazz, at least be-bop jazz, is an intellectual form. Jazz is one of the few kinds of music (like much of the classical canon) that you can't dance to. It has no steady rhythm, it plays with multiple time signatures. Be-bop is an intellectual call to arms and is obsessively dedicated to exploring form and texture. Well, so too, the exhibit.

A visit to the gift shop on the way out made everything clearer. Along with a paltry few titles taken from the enormous body of work on the history and tradition of Indian art, there were books on Native American wisdom and spirituality for sale. If that weren't bad enough, and it was, there were special displays advertising maize, sweetgrass, and sage. On the very top perched a bouquet of turkey feathers, also for sale.

No matter what the plaque said, it would be good to think about this. I have never seen, for example, during a Kandinsky exhibition, single-serving vials of vodka, babushkas, and mini-pots of caviar in the gift shop. Nor, after viewing Degas at the Met did I notice tutus, ballet shoes, baguettes, or berets next to the register. Sage and sweetgrass are, to many of us, sacred. They are sacraments. I have never seen crucifixes and wine and wafers for sale at an exhibition of Renaissance Italian art. The gifts in the Weisman gift shop were offensive and ridiculous, and the gallery should have known better, especially since the Weisman, designed by Frank Gehry, is a museum dedicated to avant-garde and experimental art. Why is it possible to frame Indian art this way? Why is it so difficult to see the art for what it really is? Intense, demanding, ironic, beautiful, accomplished conversations with Indian life.

Just as with Native American fiction, there is a tendency to read Indian artistic endeavors (whether visual or textual) as cultural products, as little dioramic pieces that describe a way of life. Indian art, or the idea that it was art, began with the collecting of objects from the material culture—parfleches, ghost shirts, pipes, pipe-bags, bandolier bags, vests, headdresses, moccasins, and so on. In many cases these things have outlived the cultures that gave them birth, and they have come to stand in for those cultures. Modern Indian art still struggles with a heavy cultural burden, so does the literature. The books are seen and treated as objects, even relics of our cultures—they are fetishized as objects that contain some essence of that culture. And maybe, since they are interpreted this way, and since they are more real, with more material reality than we have as Indians, they are linked to the idea of our disappearance. Our paintings and our books are linked to the emotional power we have over non-Indians, which is inversely proportionate to how much actual power we have in life. Perhaps the task is to make these things emote for the viewer because the viewer never felt enough or felt the right thing when there was something that could be done about our situation. To bring the intellect to bear on that sad and sordid history would be asking too much, and it might destroy the spell that binds the viewers' hearts to the idea of us. It might be much better to buy that sweetgrass, to make a smudge when you get home, to explain to your children, always in the past tense, what happened to us, who we were, where we lived, and what we thought.

Indian/Not-Indian Literature

There is probably no book about Indians that is more popular and more reviled than *The Education of Little Tree*. And, like films such as *Dirty Dancing* or *Dances with Wolves*, no one is too keen to say that they ever liked it. But the strength of these disavowals is proportionate to the strength of unstated and unrequited first love. To be reminded of an ex-lover is to be reminded of ourselves at a particular moment, to have that self locked in time and exposed when we would rather forget the whole sad affair. At least that's the way it seems to me. Falling in and out of love with people and with literature is hardly interesting—everyone does it at some point in their life. What is interesting is why and how people have fallen out of love with *Little Tree* and what that says about the interpretive practices we bring to our understanding of Native American literature.

Whether or not *Little Tree* is Indian fiction is at the root of the discomfort that the book causes. Strangely, for a long time the book was thought of as an example of Native American literature and then, overnight, it wasn't. Love or appreciation of the book was in step with its status as Indian fiction: for a long time people loved it, then love turned to hate.

It's easy to see why. When *Little Tree* was first published in 1976, this autobiographical memoir of a Cherokee boyhood convincingly (if not bathetically) evoked a specific time, had lessons to teach, and moved the reader. The book was tender in ways that other popular books about Indians were not. It was difficult to cuddle up to *Ceremony,* or *The Death of Jim Loney,* or *Winter in the Blood,* or *House Made of Dawn.* These are impressive books that challenge the reader both intellectually and aesthetically. *Little Tree,* on the other hand, written in the voice of a five-year-old protagonist, was accessible and intimate. And then, in 1991, and after it had spent a fourteen-week vacation on top of the *New York Times* Bestseller List, the news broke that *Little Tree* was a fake. The author did not have the childhood he claimed. His name was neither Little Tree nor Forrest Carter, and he was not Cherokee.

There is a long history of fake Indian texts, just as there is a long legacy of fake Indian artifacts. There is even a long history of fake Indians—people such as Grey Owl and Buffalo-Child Long Lance made careers out of their assumed identities. Adopting the "Indian pose" has been a widespread and persistent phenomenon, ranging from the forging of identity (like Forrest Carter, Grey Owl, and Long Lance) to the adoption of "worldview," to the wholesale adoration and emulation of Indian spirituality by New Agers and reformists. Even writers such as Howard

Norman have suggested that they, if not Indian by blood, are Indian by thought or allegiance.

So Forrest Carter was only one of many who had duped the reading public into thinking he was something he was not and one of many who suggested that his writing was something it was not. But, relatively speaking, he has angered more people by his forgeries than all others combined. The reason for this doesn't have as much to do with the nature of his forgery, or Forrest Carter's efforts to obscure his identity, as it does with the dark aspects of that identity. Forrest Carter was actually Asa Carter, a known Ku Klux Klan leader, a speech writer for George Wallace, and a violent man who was implicated in the castration of a slightly retarded African American in Alabama. What makes his novel so revolting to so many people is a combination of Carter's true and disturbing identity and the wholesome, sun-dappled, rosy-cheeked innocence of *Little Tree*; it is like discovering Hitler was the true author of *Old Yeller.*

Given Asa Carter's history, the volume and strength of praise for the book must have been embarrassing for some critics, especially for Native American critics such as the Abenaki translator and writer Joseph Bruchac who wrote:

> Some books can be read again and again.
> Each time they are read, it is as if something
> new has been added. Often, such books seem
> to be simply written, their story dealing with
> issues as basic as living and dying, the place of

people in the universe, the role of family and friends in the shaping of a life. *The Education of Little Tree* by the late Forrest Carter is such a book.[1]

It's hard to back up from the printed word, for better or worse it's there forever, and one can only hope that it fades away. Rennard Strickland, a lawyer of Osage and Cherokee descent, hasn't been able to escape the foreword he provided for *Little Tree*. And strangely enough, what he had to say then is even more fitting now:

> Everyone who has ever read *The Education of Little Tree* seems to remember when and where and how they came to know the book. Whether they saw it in the autobiography section of a chain bookseller; or heard it reviewed as "Book of the Week" on a television book show; or found it on the gift table at a tribal souvenir shop while passing through an Indian reservation, *Little Tree's* readers passionately remember these first meetings. For *The Education of Little Tree* is a book from which one never quite recovers. After reading *Little Tree* one never again sees the world in quite the same way.[2]

Strickland is right. No one really has recovered. The genre hasn't recovered either. And what is interesting about *Little Tree* is not that it is true (it wasn't) or

NATIVE AMERICAN FICTION: A USER'S MANUAL

that it is a fake (it was) or that its author was a terrible human being (he definitely was). What is interesting is that it was once Native American literature and now it is not. This says something about how we (readers) are trained to interpret Native American literature. We are trained to interpret the genre the same way we were encouraged to "read" the exhibit of Native art at the Weisman Museum: with our hearts, not with our heads. It also proves that the words and images, the literary work in Native American literature, takes a backseat to issues of identity and perceived "authenticity."

Little Tree particularly incensed Sherman Alexie, a very vocal critic of Indian imposters. So much so that the chapter "Introduction to Native American Literature" in his novel *Indian Killer* is partially devoted to a discussion of *Little Tree*. Marie, an Indian activist, has arrived at her first day of class and is immediately upset by the reading list:

> While Marie was surprised by the demographics of the class, she was completely shocked by the course reading list. One of the books, *The Education of Little Tree,* was supposedly written by a Cherokee Indian named Forrest Carter. But Forrest Carter was actually the pseudonym for a former Grand Wizard of the Ku Klux Klan. (. . .)
>
> After seeing the reading list, Marie knew that Dr. Mather was full of shit.[3]

After a number of pages in which Alexie sets up white characters only to knock them down, Marie and her professor exchange views on the role of Indian literature itself. Professor Mather defends the presence of Jack Wilson (a mystery novelist whose identity in the real world as Tony Hillerman Alexie barely bothers to disguise) by saying that he gives an accurate portrayal of Indian life. Marie responds:

> "How can Wilson present an authentic
> and traditional view of the Indian world if
> he isn't authentic and traditional himself?"
> asked Marie. "I mean, I've done some research
> on this guy. He isn't even Indian at all. How
> would he know about the despair, or happiness, in the Indian world?"[4]

Alexie seems to believe that the role of literature is to represent. As such a writer, he believes that one must experience pain and despair and happiness in order to recreate it on the page. And, significantly, in order to represent or discuss Indian life one needs to be Indian. With that in mind, Alexie's vehemence is particularly interesting when you realize that *Little Tree* is a close cousin—thematically, stylistically, and structurally—to Alexie's novels.

Little Tree and *Indian Killer,* though *Reservation Blues* might be a better fit, are novels of education. However, in each case, the person being educated is not the main character. It is the reader who is being

NATIVE AMERICAN FICTION: A USER'S MANUAL

taught. These are not bildungsromans, they are culture manuals.

The Education of Little Tree begins when Little Tree's mother dies. His father had run off long before. After the funeral, his extended family argues over his mother's meager possessions, and Little Tree is taken in by his grandparents. He is brought to live with them in their backwoods cabin where he spends the next four years of his life "learning" how to be Cherokee until his grandparents die and Little Tree heads west. During those four years Little Tree gets taller, he gets stronger, he can read better and, as times passes, it isn't as hard for him to walk with his grandpa to the crossroads store to "sell their wares." But there is very little plot. The best plot description of *Little Tree* would be: after the death of his parents a young Cherokee boy comes to live with his grandparents, who, despite increasing pressure from the outside world, try to teach him the way of his ancestors in the time before they die.

Little Tree doesn't have much of a plot, and it doesn't contain any development either. Little Tree has the same intellect, same voice, and same disposition when he walks out of the mountains as he did when he walked in. There was, of course, material knowledge and cultural insight passed on to Little Tree, but these were put on with as much ease as he dons his deerskin shirt and moccasins on his second day in the mountains—and as easily taken off. Throughout, the boy underneath remains the same. There was no transformation in Little Tree, no crisis of character, no moment of doubt, no test of his knowledge.

Instead, there are episodes. These episodes, linked and laid out chronologically, provide the structure of the novel. The episodes or scenes range from the mental, through the menial, to the physically sublime. Little Tree learns, in the span of one short conversation, his first, with his grandpa, the "Way" of the Cherokee. Which is really a folksy version of Social Darwinism—the weak are killed by the strong and it is a good thing because if the weak were allowed to breed they . . .

From there Little Tree is introduced to a Cherokee version of fox hunting in which the fox doesn't die; he learns of the Trail of Tears; he learns to make whiskey; not to trade with a Christian; how to love; what it means to belong someplace; and that, eventually, it all ends. Through all of this, even though Little Tree says he has learned something, his knowledge is hardly the point. Little Tree is merely a cipher through which Indian knowledge and a nostalgia for an Indian past can be passed on to the reader. The reader, not Little Tree, emerges changed. The reader has new ideas and knowledge.

Reservation Blues has a different structure than *Little Tree*—more plot-based—and the characters do evolve to a slightly greater degree. But, like Carter, Alexie isn't interested in portraying movement or change as much as he is interested in recreating or illuminating a condition.

Reservation Blues focuses on the hopes and dreams (literally) of a band of Indians who want to become rock stars. Victor, Junior, Thomas, Chess, and Checkers, aided by a mystical guitar and a mystical mother figure, try to launch their careers in spite of, and in the face of, historical racism and internalized patterns of failure. That the group fails hardly matters. They, in Alexie's words "were alive; they'd keep living. They sang together with the shadow horses: we are alive, we'll keep living."[5] What does seem to matter is the process of education, which in every instance follows the same pattern: a white person does something stupid, which is racialized as "white behavior," and the Indian characters react, sometimes in thought, sometimes in dialogue, and at other times, though rarely, in action. The true beneficiary of these conflicts is the reader, just as in *Little Tree*. It is the reader who is educated.

The first "lesson" for the reader occurs a few pages into the book when the mystic mother, aptly named Big Mom, hears gunshots. She runs from her house in time to witness the massacre of Indian horses:

> she saw the future and the past, the white soldiers in blue uniforms with black rifles and pistols. She saw the Indian horses shot and fallen like tattered sheets. Big Mom stood on the rise and watched the horses fall, until only one remained.
>
> Big Mom watched the Indian colt circled by soldiers. The colt darted from side to side, looked for escape. One soldier, an officer, stepped down from his pony, walked over to the colt, gently touched its face, and

whispered in its ear. The colt shivered as the officer put his pistol between its eyes and pulled the trigger.[6]

This scene of slaughter—outside time and even tense—leads to an Indian reaction. Big Mom buries the horses, but takes a rib bone from one and makes a flute from it. She uses this flute every morning "to remind everybody that music created and recreated the world daily."[7] While this sentiment is beautiful, it is not true of the world of *Reservation Blues*. That world is made up out of white transgression and Indian reaction, and the dialectic leads to educational synthesis. Again, the readership is being educated, not the characters. As in *Little Tree,* there is no sense of transformation or change. The characters make better choices or different choices than they did in the beginning, but they don't change as characters. What is so exciting about Alexie's writing is that, what should feel static, doesn't. He expertly creates a sense of motion—through plot and, more importantly, through his manipulation of icons and stereotypes—in spite of the characters' inertia. There is a marked difference between *Reservation Blues* and *Little Tree.* Whereas the end of *Little Tree* is glum and hopeless—there is no Nation, the narrator tells us upon arriving in Oklahoma—Alexie *is* able to infuse a sense of hope in his text. The hope is derived from a wholesale rejection of white people. Thomas comes to the realization that his life goal is to have brown-faced children:

NATIVE AMERICAN FICTION: A USER'S MANUAL

"Thomas," Chess said and took his hand, "let's get married. Let's have kids."

Thomas was surprised. He couldn't respond.

"Really," Chess said. "Let's have lots of brown babies. I want my babies to look up and see two brown faces. That's the best thing we can give them, enit? Two brown faces. Do you want to?"

Thomas smiled.

"Okay," he said.[8]

The very fabric of Alexie's novel is bent to the task of illuminating the Indian condition. It is the Indian condition and statements that "educate" us about its dimensions that provide most of the humor, and even the texture of reality, in Alexie's writing. For instance, after Victor smashes Thomas's guitar in front of the trading post, Thomas "started to cry. That was the worst thing an Indian man could do if he were sober. A drunk Indian can cry and sing into his beer all night long, and the rest of the drunk Indians will sing backup."[9] The education offered by *Reservation Blues* is a curriculum designed for the outsider—this is why concepts like "snagging" and food like fry-bread are explained in such curious detail and why the very qualities of reservation life are qualified so completely:

The word *gone* echoed all over the reservation. The reservation was gone itself, just a shell of its former self, just a fragment of the whole. But the reservation still possessed power and rage, magic and loss, joys and jealousy. The reservation tugged at the lives of its Indians, stole from them in the middle of the night, watched impassively as the horses and salmon disappeared.[10]

But *Little Tree* and *Reservation Blues* share more than just educational narratives. They are also united stylistically and thematically. For starters, there is a marked lack of the kind of figurative language we see in Silko, Welch, and Erdrich, although there are moments when each book reaches for just such language. Carter, for his part, hoards his similes only to squander them in order to animate the natural world. It's a time-tried-and-true device, almost an obligation, to try and give a little "lift" to natural expression: "The sun hit the top [of the mountain] like an explosion, sending showers of glitter and sparkle into the air. . . . And now the mountain popped and gave breathing sighs that sent little puffs of steam into the air."[11] The simile is awkward and doesn't really make sense—the sun does not "hit *like* an explosion." It could "explode *off* the mountain" or "explode *on* the mountaintop" but it cannot hit *like* an explosion; explosions are sometimes the result of an impact, not the other way around. Alexie is also guilty of the same kind of infelicities when he reaches for figurative language. When Robert Johnson shows up on the reservation and speaks to Thomas, "his words sounded like stones in his mouth and coals in his stomach."[12]

How can "his words sound like coals in his stomach"? There are more problems with the prose than just his similes: "There, she [Big Mom] saw the future and the past, the white soldiers in blue uniforms with black rifles and pistols. She saw the Indian horses shot and fallen like tattered sheets."[13] Are the horses shot like sheets? If so, how and when are sheets shot? Or have they fallen like sheets (they would have to die gauzily for this to be true)? Or, is Alexie trying to say that they were draped here and there on the ground? Further on we are told that Junior had hair that was so long he "could have donated yards of the stuff and made a fortune."[14] But most of us have yet to make a fortune giving things away for free. If that were the case, Indians would be rich. It is as if both writers felt that since they were writers, they were obligated to use fancy language, but, after having tried it, they realized they didn't have the taste for it. And what readers think of as lyrical language is not language at all. Rather, "beauty" is the aftertaste left by their own emotional reactions to the stories in front of them.

Aside from these mercifully brief attempts at precious language, *Little Tree* and *Reservation Blues* both use an active and amazing literary device. Hyperbole. It is the best literary device in the whole wide world. It is striking the degree to which both of these books use hyperbole—sanctioned exaggeration—to make delicate points about loss and pain. In *Reservation Blues,* we are struck immediately by Alexie's reliance on the device. "As she stepped out of her front door, Big Mom heard the first gunshot, which reverberated in her DNA."[15] What Alexie wants to communicate is that the shot was powerful, and it hurt, and he achieves this, not by understatement, but by way of overstatement. Further on, when Junior drinks a beer he drains it "like a pumpkin that dropped off the World Trade Center and landed on the head of a stockbrocker."[16] [Pumpkins are drained? Pumpkins drop off the WTC—like "reservation strange fruit"? Or they are dropped off?] He uses the same device for humor, not just for emotional effect. The man who might be Sioux at the trading post "had cheekbones so big that he knocked people over when he moved his head from side to side."[17] The effect of these freshman attempts at humor and poetry is a complicated blend of anger, humor, educational material, and, above all—an atmosphere of earnest innocence.

Carter manipulates the semblance of innocence through a kind of caricature as well. Little Tree, having just arrived at age five to live with his grandparents, says that he had trouble keeping up with his grandfather (whose height is listed in the beginning as six foot four). "I reckin I was little for my age (five going on six) [he tells us] for the top of my head come just above Granpa's knees, and I was always in a continual trot behind him."[18] Little Tree would not just have to be little to be knee-height at age five—he would have to be a dwarf or a midget. There are other instances throughout the book that, when looked at closely, defy belief: a spider using a fern as a trampoline,

Little Tree and Grandpa laughing until they almost fell off the mountain . . .

To ask hard questions about language in books praised for their "lyricality" and "narrative power" and "poetic representation" is not out of bounds. And to call attention to mealy prose and tortured sentences is not to be perversely literal. To do so is to ask what language is doing and how it contributes to meaning. If Alexie's sentences don't work, then what does? If Alexie's and Carter's books don't derive their power from beauty or from beautiful and well-crafted prose (and it cannot be claimed that either book is beautiful or well-crafted), then where do they get their power? The answer lies in their use of hyperbole and the way they mobilize stock images that have come to inform Native American literature from European writers like Rousseau, Voltaire, Chateaubriand, and Walter Scott who crossed the Atlantic, took up residence with Americans such as James Fenimore Cooper and William Gilmore Simms, and were then channeled through Longfellow and Whitman and Washington Irving and on down the line. But first, back to hyperbole.

These exaggerations, these instances of hyperbole, provide humor and they transform the commonplace, or what could be seen as commonplace, into the epic. Hyperbole in literature is not a desperate last resort, as it often is in conversation. Prose, in general (and this line of thought goes back to Aristotle), is imitative. It imitates states of being and transforms them through language. Fresh language can keep prose from being prosaic. That is, it can save the story from being commonplace. In the absence of fresh or artful language, hyperbole becomes *the thing* that elevates these books, and it becomes *the thing* because it contributes to the humor found in both stories. The misproportions that hyperbole occasions, hyperbole as a distorting lens, save both texts from being mere lifestyle manuals and enable us to laugh at things we would usually take very seriously—Indian drinking, racism, death, the disappearance of Indian lifeways, and so on. What Alexie and Carter have created are not Vermeers as much as Warhols. Exaggeration is their only virtue. They are grotesque and tender at the same time. It is a very short step from Warhol to Rockwell. Both are comedic and touching.

Comedy, we are reminded in Aristotle's *Poetics,*

> is an imitation of men worse than the average; worse, however, not as regards any and every sort of fault, but only as regards one particular kind, the Ridiculous, which is a species of the Ugly. The Ridiculous may be defined as a mistake or deformity not productive of pain or harm to others; the mask, for instance, that excites laughter, is something ugly and distorted without causing pain.[19]

In the case of *Reservation Blues* and *The Education of Little Tree,* it is not the characters, not the Indian characters, anyway, who seem ridiculous—they are rendered tenderly, as if off limits for ridicule—rather, the world in which we find them, the situations and the description of Indian action, is ridiculed. The

NATIVE AMERICAN FICTION: A USER'S MANUAL

hyperbolic prose is commensurate with the despera-
tion present in these lives. Both books distort and, in
the end, dehumanize white characters. They exagger-
ate one or two qualities (sexual rapacity in the case
of Father Arnold and, in the scene when Little Tree
gets slickered out of fifty cents, white fiscal double-
dealing) in order to provide both comedy and dramatic tension. I say dehumanized not because either
book is particularly unjust in its depiction of white
cultures, but because the humanity of the white characters is of no importance whatsoever. What is important is the trait or habit of cultural interaction,
which can always be identified with racism, that
gets extracted from the white character and put on
display.

These two books create, through language, the
same kind of narrative qualities present in Michael
Moore's documentaries: they are burlesques that somehow manage to educate us, entertain us, and make us
laugh. At the core, there is a sensitive primal value
(Indian life? liberal consciousness?) that is being pro-
tected by all the antics that surround them.

These books are effective because of the relationship
they create between humor and hyperbole. But they
are deadly because of how they create new kinds
of racial typing. In each case, though in different
ways, Indian life and white life are portrayed as being
incommensurate.

For Little Tree, what can be considered "white life"
ends for him when his mother dies and he goes to live
with his grandparents. As a child who is mixed, it is

crucial the reader see the shift in allegiance from white culture to Indian. This happens on the second page of the book when Little Tree and his grandparents board the bus on their way back to the mountains.

> The bus driver told Granpa how much it was and while Granpa counted out the money real careful—for the light wasn't good to count by—the bus driver turned around to the crowd in the bus and lifted his right hand and said, *"How!"* and laughed, and all the people laughed. I felt better about it, knowing they was friendly and didn't take offense because we didn't have a ticket.[20]

Little Tree has effectively switched over. He is grouped with his grandparents by the people on the bus, he is interpreted through them. And the reader is encouraged to see Little Tree as Indian; that is, as possessing positive value in contrast to the nameless and anonymous white folks around him.

Two pages later, as they walk the trail to his grandparents' cabin, he hears his grandmother humming and Little Tree remarks, "I knew it was Indian, and needed no words for its meaning to be clear, and it made me feel safe."[21] So, in addition to being interpreted by outsiders as Indian, Little Tree himself claims allegiance by way of insider knowledge and understanding. However, in order to seal his place and his identity, Little Tree needs to be validated by the authentic Indians in the book. It is from his grandmother, on the very next page, that he receives his patent of Indian authenticity. Having arrived at his grandparents' shack that day, his grandmother sings to him as he is being put to bed:

"They now have sensed him coming
The forest and the wood-wind
Father mountain makes him welcome with his song.
They have no fear of Little Tree
They know his heart is kindness
And they sing, 'Little tree [sic] is not alone.'"[22]

Little Tree has been recognized by nature herself and has received that most precious of things, an Indian name. He has, in the span of three short pages, become Indian:

> Granma sang and rocked slowly back and forth. And I could hear the wind talking, and Lay-nah, the spring branch, singing about me and telling all my brothers.
>
> I knew I was Little Tree, and I was happy that they loved me and wanted me. And so I slept, and I did not cry.[23]

With his identity firmly in place Little Tree is now licensed to show the distinctions between white ways and Indian ways. It matters little that Indians and whites, and Cherokees in particular, have been in contact and trade, have had social and sexual intercourse, and have to some extent blended religions for over four hundred years. In this book it is as if that has never been the case.

INDIAN/NOT-INDIAN LITERATURE

This is why the book can, without blushing, make claims about the difference between Indian understanding and white misunderstanding, about the tragic difference between Indian and white thought. A good example is when Little Tree and his grandfather, having risen before dawn, watch the sun come up. They are able to say "she's coming alive" and then claim, even though the reader—no matter what race he or she might be—is *fully* able to understand the idea, that "me and Granpa had us an understanding that most folks didn't know."[24] Just as, further on, Little Tree distinguishes between white and Indian thinking:

> Granpa was half Scot, but he thought Indian. Such seemed to be the case with others, like the great Red Eagle, Bill Weatherford, or Emperor McGilvery or McIntosh. They gave themselves, as the Indian did, to nature, not trying to subdue it, or pervert it, but to live with it. And so they loved the thought, and loving it grew to be it, so that they could not think as the white man.[25]

The effect of these false distinctions between Indian and white seems to be, by devaluing one way of living and thinking and elevating the other, to make Indian experiences all the more precious and unique. Thus Carter has no need for "beautiful" or posed language. Language is not the vehicle used to arrive at meaning. Carter has expertly manipulated the tried-and-true ways of understanding Indian thought and culture (living with nature not against it, seeing nature as alive and beautiful not as a resource to be exploited) to do the heavy lifting for his book.

Alexie does the same thing, though in his books, there is no sense of *becoming* Indian. That is impossible, and not only that, it is somehow, in Alexie's world, immoral. *Reservation Blues* is laced with anxiety about transformation, shared understanding, and racial pollution. The degree to which racial impurity is an active force in *Reservation Blues* is equaled only in Cooper's Leatherstocking stories. In both books the mixed-blood characters, or those who promote racial mixing, die terrible deaths. Uncas and Cora have a love connection, and they are punished for it. But there is even something residually sexual about their deaths: Le Subtil "sheaths" his knife in Cora's bosom and then passes his knife "three several times" into Uncas's "bosom." In *Reservation Blues,* Junior, who we learn has had a child with a white woman, is a miserable failure in everything except his own death, which he expertly pulls off with a stolen rifle on top of a water tower. The Leatherstocking himself, a mean self-promoter, whenever his abilities are on display, is anxious to remind his companions (a little too stridently, a little too nervously) that he is "a white man without a cross [meaning his blood is not mixed]."[26] In *Reservation Blues* the character most interested in racial purity is Chess, who thinks,

> "The fractions will take over," she thinks.
> "Your half-blood son will have quarter-blood children and eighth-blood grandchildren, and

INDIAN/NOT-INDIAN LITERATURE

then they won't be Indians anymore. . . . Those
quarter-blood and eighth-blood grandchildren
will find out they're Indian and torment the
rest of us real Indians."[27]

This sentiment is crude, reductive, uncharitable,
ignorant (ignorant of culture, language, ceremony,
and community), and essentialist. And it is completely understandable. After a novel that documents
the inroads whites and white culture have made
on Indian life, land, and consciousness; after almost
300 pages in which whiteness itself (like that of the
whale) is cast as evil, and happiness, success, talent,
and luck are scrubbed clean of color and white-
washed; after all that, what else can Chess or anyone
do that is not tainted with whiteness? Making brown
babies is the logical end point of the novel. And it
highlights the clear and final racial distinctions at
work in the book.

From the start of the novel, there is the world . . .
and then there is the reservation. When Robert Johnson arrives in Wellpinit on the first page of the novel
the "entire reservation knew about the black man
five minutes after he showed up at the crossroads.
All the Spokanes thought up reasons to leave work
or home . . ."[28] The *entire reservation,* and *all the
Spokanes*—this is a crucial first step for the novel.
The otherness here is complete. When Johnson
comments on the natural beauty of the reservation,
Thomas is quick to imply that Johnson can't really
see what Indian life, what the reservation, is really
like:

"This is a beautiful place," Johnson said.

"But you haven't seen everything," Thomas said.

"What else is there?"

Thomas thought about all the dreams that were murdered here, and the bones buried quickly just inches below the surface, all waiting to break through the foundations of those government houses. (. . .)

"There's a whole lot you haven't seen," Thomas said.[29]

It is on the next page that Alexie suggests, creates, and enforces the complete difference between authentic Indian life and the rest of the world, and he does it with a single word. Reservation.

Thomas watched Johnson walk up the mountain until he was out of vision [out of sight?] and beyond any story. Then Thomas saw the guitar, Robert Johnson's guitar, lying on the floor of the van. Thomas picked it up, strummed the strings, felt a small pain in the palms of his hands, and heard the first sad note of the reservation blues.[30]

From that point on, without ever really defining what reservation means except to imply that it means Indian and Indian means reservation in a dizzying tautological duet, the divisions between what is and what is not Indian are absolutely clear. We are told about "reservation appetizers" and "reservation roads" and "reservation love songs" and "reservation cars" and "reservation magician" and "reservation clown" and "reservation romances" and "reservation high school dance" and "reservation divas," among others. The effect creates value (ironically: value through destitution and desuetude) for Indian life and devalues white culture. What remains is multicultural zero sum gain.

In *Little Tree,* when Little Tree learns, the reader learns along with him. When Little Tree *becomes,* the reader also *becomes.* Whereas Alexie does something much more complicated. He invites the reader to learn whenever the narrative stops and the characters discourse, but by attaching the adjectival "reservation" to the objects in these lessons, he simultaneously holds the reader outside the reservation. Alexie weaves a wonderful cloth out of education and rejection. And it is through this contrast that meaning is generated; his story can be specific and—by mobilizing a similar but slightly different set of ideas about Indians (the alcohol, the government handouts, the traditions, the very fact of difference itself)—universal at the same time.

There are other similarities between *Little Tree* and *Reservation Blues,* but these are affinities they share with many other Native American novels. The points of comparison, the sheer number of them, are stunning:

- *The Education of Little Tree, Reservation Blues, Ceremony, Love Medicine, House*

Made of Dawn, and *Little,* among others, have central characters who are orphans.

- In each case the main character (Tayo or Abel or Thomas) has been orphaned and usually raised by a grandparent or cluster of aunts and uncles.
- The generation skipping that takes place as a result of the orphanizing process is linked, thematically, to the central characters' relationship with and distance from the community, culture, and tribe.
- In each case, the absence of parents makes literal, and immediately compelling, the search for connection.
- Also, in the novels that have characters who are either overtly spiritual—like Betonie in *Ceremony,* Big Mom in *Reservation Blues,* and Mik-Api in *Fools Crow*—or, barring spiritualism, are culturally central, or authentically and uncomplicatedly Indian (Willow John in *Little Tree,* and Eli in *Love Medicine*), the spiritual or cultural person is, geographically, located far from the center of the village or the action of the novel. They exist on the fringes of the novel-map, as if to be spiritual or culturally authentic is necessarily to be out of time and out of touch (with Betonie being the one complicated instance of this); as if to exist in their spiritual capacity they cannot be in daily contact with modernity, which itself is a trauma visited on Indian people in novels.

- In the novels listed above and in others not listed, there is a clear division made between the land and urban landscapes, between the reservation and the city. In each and every case the city is a place where Indians go to be injured, both physically and psychically. Ultimately, they come face to face with themselves in the city, almost as though the city were one big bottle of booze in which they climb and hit rock bottom, only to climb up and out and back to the reservation where, after they have been tested and tried, they truly reconnect to their culture, families, and selves.

- None of the central characters in any of these novels (Fools Crow being the obvious exception) speak their native language. And if they have the ability to speak their language, because of multiple traumas such as war experiences, witchery, physical injury, and guilt (for Abel and Tayo in particular), their languages are unavailable to them and so they don't speak them. The distance the characters are from their native languages signifies the distance they need to cover or recover in order to be healed.

- Speaking of healing, there is, at the end of each and every one of these novels an almost-happy ending: an ending that is hopeful if not happy. What we have is a mixture of relief, hope, and pain that, when

it's all over, resolves into satisfaction with
survival and continuance, if not happiness. What readers seem to want and the
Native American context can provide is the
ultimate evolution of American literature,
a kind of literature satisfying to everyone:
tragedies with happy endings.

To make lists like the one above is not to suggest
that all Indian novels are the same, or so similar as to
seem the same. And it would be a mistake to suggest
that all these novels share most of their key elements
and to stop probing into the books' inner and minute
workings. To list attributes is not to investigate. But
it is important to recover books that have been cast
down and are no longer part of the heavenly Indian
host; books that have been cast out solely on the basis
of authorship and identity. After all, what kind of genre
do we (as readers, writers, and Indians) have when
books that are made out of the same exact cloth, that
use the same images in the same way, that manipu-
late the mythology and sense around Indian identity in identical ways, and have the same or similar
prose styles are not grouped together only or merely
because one author is white and another is Indian?
At best, writers and critics have created a new kind
of essentialism and at worst have perpetuated a new
kind of textual racism. And gone is any sense that literature has the power to create the world anew.

To recover books like *Little Tree* is not to say that
authorship or authorial identity doesn't matter. It

does. It matters especially in the case of Indian fiction and in Indian writing more largely construed. We have, for so long, been spoken for—by folklorists, linguists, anthropologists, apologists, environmentalists, New Agers, and the liberal left—and not given the chance to speak for ourselves. Or, if we have spoken for ourselves (and writers such as Charles Eastman and William Warren *have* spoken for us in their own way), we have had to speak in very specific and debilitating ways in order to escape the stories, the very iron bars of our cage, that have been created for us.

Even so, it is crucial to recover books like *Little Tree,* and to see it as "Indian" as *Reservation Blues.* By exiling *Little Tree* we are damning ourselves and our efforts to an endless and agonizing game of identity politics and strivings for personal, authorial authenticity. To ignore the links that *Little Tree* has with other Indian novels (and as a piece of writing, and this was the point of this essay, it is as Indian as any other Indian novel) is to weaken our novels and our criticism. If we do ignore it, we are committing the sin of not treating literature as literature. We are, in effect, saying that writing doesn't matter. It's unavoidable in a way—the puppeteer will always be more interesting than the puppets he wields precisely *because* we can't know why and how they move the strings. The issue of authenticity is compelling because we can't ever really know who or what is authentic, and the rules and values shift as soon as we think we do know. But it would be crazy as well as dismally adult to say that we should watch the puppet show or interpret the puppets based on where the puppeteer grew up or whether he's had a bad day, or by what his desires are.

Little Tree might be able to educate us after all. By reading it intelligently we can see that the identity of the author is less important than the fact that many authors create identities for themselves that have little to do with what or how they really think or where and how they actually grew up. By reading *Little Tree* as Indian literature, we can think effectively about the power that identity confers on authors and how that authority is constituted.

On that note, life and literature seem committed to offering up opportunities to inspect the issues of culture, identity, and authority in equal measure to our willingness to miss those opportunities. On 23 January 2006, in the shadow of the dazzlingly lit drama of James Frey's *A Million Little Pieces,* another play about imposture and exaggeration opened off-off-Broadway in the *LA Weekly* about the Indian writer who called himself Nasdijj.

In a wonderful article entitled "Navahoax" by Matthew Fleischer, a dazed reading public (surely not as dazed as the editorial public) learned that the best-selling Indian memoirist and nonfiction writer Nasdijj, who, beginning in 1999 wrote three memoirs in short succession, was not Indian; he did not adopt a baby boy with fetal alcohol syndrome, and he did not have a life anything like the one he garnered so much acclaim writing about.[31] Nasdijj is Tim Barrus, a gay, Anglo writer from Michigan. Suddenly, weirdly, the claims for the brilliancy of Nasdijj's writing seem a little thin. "An authentic, important book... unfailingly honest and very nearly perfect," wrote *Esquire*. "This is a fascinating book," Ted Conover crowed in the *New York Times*, "unlike anything you are likely to have read."[32] And the *Minneapolis Star Tribune* chimed in agreement: "A memoir of survival... the flat-out best nonfiction writing of the year."[33] And what's strange about all of this is that when one picks up Nasdijj's writing now, it sounds (regardless of Nasdijj's origins and ethnicity) trite and packaged and shallow and full of the kinds of clichés that always waft from bad writing about Indians like the stink coming off a corpse. Such as: "Death, to the Navajo, is like the cold wind that blows across the mesa from the north..." You get the idea.

What's especially weird is that "authentic" Native American writer Sherman Alexie, who played a part in the exposé, was tipped off to Nasdijj not because Nasdijj didn't sound Indian but because he did. Alexie is quoted in the *LA Weekly* as saying "The whole time I was reading I was thinking, this doesn't just sound like me, this is me." And that, "at first I was flattered but as I kept reading I noticed he was borrowing from other Native writers too. I thought, this can't be real."[34]

The weirdness in all of this has largely been missed. Nasdijj seems to have tipped his hand by sounding like the Indian writer most obsessed with authenticity, who, more than any other Native writer, bases his legitimacy on his own Indianness. What should Native writing sound like if not other writing about Indians? It is truly ironic that Nasdijj tried to sound

NATIVE AMERICAN FICTION: A USER'S MANUAL

like Alexie (and did not) who tries to sound like, in some ways, Cervantes, Marquez, and Voltaire (but cannot). What ultimately should sound less authentic? A writer who tries to sound like other Native writers or a writer who tries to sound like other non-Native writers?

That yet again another writer posed as an Indian tells us nothing other than the fact that Indianness is still a stage worth performing on. What *is* telling is what kind of Indian Nasdijj felt he had to be in order to be authentic. He did not pose as an Indian accountant living in the suburbs of Phoenix. He did not pose as a Cherokee contractor building parking ramps in Oklahoma City. He did not (god forbid) pretend to be a happy, healthy, well-adjusted Ojibwe writer from Minnesota dividing his time between Minneapolis and Leech Lake Reservation . . . no. He felt somehow that to be an "authentic" Indian he needed to be the kind of Indian we see in Sherman Alexie's prose inventions. He needed to be Sherman's kind of Indian. That *does* tell us something about Nasdijj as both an audience member (reading fiction as real) and a player (playing Indian for other readers). And it tells us something about how Alexie's writing is perceived as "true" and the rather deadly social needs fiction can be rigged up to meet.

It isn't shocking that an opportunist and bad artist like Nasdijj borrowed some of his pale fire from Alexie, Michael Dorris, Momaday, and the rest. As we have seen, there is a long, rich, interesting history of Indian fakes. What is shocking is that his perceived Indianness obscured truly bad writing, written in bad faith and even worse taste. I don't know if frauds like Nasdijj hurt "real" Indian citizens any more than non-frauds do. It does hurt other Native writers though, most of whom don't stand a chance of writing for *Esquire* or being reviewed in the *Times* unless they lard their prose (as do Nasdijj and Alexie and Carter) with perceived Indianisms and authenticating marks, with Indian tears and the bones of the ancestors and the cold sharp wind off the mesas. Nasdijj and Alexie and Carter all use the mark of authenticity to provide much of their magic—that two of them are frauds and one of them is not does matter, just not quite as much as the fact that of the three Alexie is the best writer. The hoax and subsequent discussions around it hurt Indian writers twice over because the debate about hoaxes has once again focused on identity not writing, and those who were hoaxed will now require even more proof of cultural citizenship and the magic, mirage-like, wavering, and complicated bounds of culture will be patrolled even more vigilantly thereby defining Indianness even more narrowly and rigidly. What the Nasdijj drama should show us if we tried to think about it productively is that by foregrounding authenticity we treat Native American fictions as artifacts, not art; fictions animated by what we imagine to be the origins of the author, not the originality of the writing.

This reminds me of a fascinating and sad story about Charlemagne, related by Italo Calvino in his brilliant essay "Quickness."

Late in life the emperor Charlemagne fell in love with a German girl. The barons at his court were extremely worried when they saw that the sovereign, wholly taken up with his amorous passion and unmindful of his regal dignity, was neglecting the affairs of state. When the girl suddenly died, the courtiers were greatly relieved—but not for long, because Charlemagne's love did not die with her. The emperor had the embalmed body carried to his bedchamber, where he refused to be parted from it. The Archbishop Turpin, alarmed by this macabre passion, suspected an enchantment and insisted on examining the corpse. Hidden under the girl's dead tongue he found a ring with a precious stone set in it. As soon as the ring was in Turpin's hands, Charlemagne fell passionately in love with the archbishop and hurriedly had the girl buried. In order to escape the embarrassing situation, Turpin flung the ring into Lake Constance. Charlemagne thereupon fell in love with the lake and would not leave its shores.[35]

Charlemagne—despite his abilities and his intelligence—is not enchanted by his beloved's beauty, or by the archbishop, or by the beautiful waters of Lake Constance. The ring binds his interest to them. It is much the same for readers, critics, and writers of Indian fiction: often they may think they are enchanted with the writing, when it is the perceived authenticity of the author to which they are drawn. And just as Charlemagne cannot realize his error—mistaking a live thing for something dead—and persists, when confronted with reality, in switching his passion to whatever vessel contains the ring, readers of Indian fiction are magnetized by authority and instead of reevaluating what draws them to the literature, they simply, when confronted by the true identity of someone like Forrest Carter, switch their gaze to the next enchanted object. All the while our books suffer and rot. Worse than that, we (readers) are in danger of mistaking a dead thing—like the received ideas, stale prose, commonplace realizations, essentialist projects, and racial anxiety that make up books like *The Education of Little Tree* and *Reservation Blues*—for something alive and rich and worthy of our attention.

"The real protagonist of the story," writes Calvino, "is the magic ring, because it is the movements of the ring that determine those of the characters and because it is the ring that establishes the relationship between them."[36] The ring is the narrative link that binds the different aspects and episodes of the stories together. It is sad to think that authorial authority and identity are the ring that holds Indian fiction together.

It would be good to remember that we (readers) aren't convinced by a book like *Reservation Blues* or *The Education of Little Tree* because we know what the author's experience or background is. It would be good to remember that we don't enjoy stories with the text of the story on one side of the page and the author's vita on the other (or perhaps, in the current habit of reading for cultural truth we actually do read this way). It would be good to remember that it is the prose that convinces us of its own authenticity. And if it doesn't, it should. We don't, after all, believe in characters, images, or situations because they *are* authentic. We believe them because they *seem* authentic. And it is the seemingness of literature that is interesting—where language meets and dances with belief.

Some Final Thoughts about the Non-Existence of Native American Fiction

This book has been written with the narrow conviction that if Native American literature is worth thinking about at all, it is worth thinking about as literature. And these essays also betray a much broader conviction: Native American fiction does not exist.

Much energy and effort has been expended thinking about the first two words of the troika—NATIVE and AMERICAN, but little, in comparison, about the third—LITERATURE. As it stands, the vast majority of thought that has been poured onto Native American literature has puddled, for the most part, on how the texts are positioned in relation to history or culture and can be summed up as follows:

1. Native American literature contains within it links to culturally generated forms of storytelling.

2. Native American literature reflects the experience of Native Americans in the United States.

3. Native American literature acts out, by virtue of its cultural material, a tribally inflected, ancient form of "postmodern" discourse.

If there was such a thing as Native American fiction, one would think that the criticism would show more interest in literature. Naturally, certain so-called Native American novels make use of the idea of storytelling, and storytelling has become an interesting *subject* of fiction by and about Native Americans, but the simple fact is that not all stories are novels. And even though many of the novels treated here can be thought of as instances of "historical or ethical documentation," the novel is or should be, in the end, the object of study, not the historical record.[1] As for the third, and most ridiculous, assertion that Native American literature is itself "postmodern" commentary, it follows that if this is the case, we first have to treat novels as literary creations, not as spontaneous expressions of critical solidarity or relevance. By far the most amazing thing about Native American literature is the reluctance of its creators and commentators to treat it as literature that exists within a field of other literatures. What has remained a popular position is to think of literature as located within the sphere of life. It is not.

The phrase we hear so often that always begins

NATIVE AMERICAN FICTION: A USER'S MANUAL

"where I come from, stories . . ." needs to be questioned. It needs to be questioned because, despite claims for the power and efficacy for stories (made by Silko and Momaday and Erdrich), the suggestion of place and the imposition of personality come first in that construction: Where. I. Come from. Instead of basing our analysis on the first four words of that phrase, we should take a close look at the fifth. Stories. In this case, novels. If novels say anything, they say it as text, and as such, the first step is to look closely at the words that comprise those texts and to move, ever slowly, ever outward, from there. This book is meant to be that first step.

What makes the intelligent interrogation of Native American literature difficult is the degree to which the literature has become a central part of an argument about authenticity. And to suggest, as some of these essays have suggested, that the elements with which the novels treated here are constructed, even though they might look Indian or seem cultural, are not in service to, and do not come from, "the culture." The same dilemma can be found in the issue of authenticity in art. The anxiety around the authenticity of this or that painting has more to do with the owner's material investment in the piece and the feeling of owning something truly unique than with artistry or art itself. We would never pay $43 million for a copy of a van Gogh, even if it were a perfect copy. What we want in art is THE original, if we can afford it. What we want in Native American fiction is fiction that is "authentically" Indian. And we're willing to be duped again and again by claims of authenticity just to feel like we've gotten "the real thing."

To claim, as I have, that some aspects of these novels—the use of myth, the perspective from "inside" the culture—have been misconstrued by readers and writers alike is not to engage in an argument about whether the writers or the books are or aren't authentic. That question remains open if you're interested in that question. I have striven to show the power of the literary, the power of the imaginary, to create semblances of culture. And I have tried to expose the sentiments that drive the desire for culture—in the novels and in their interpretation.

I think it is safe to say that Native American literature has never been taken very seriously as literature. And this, if nothing else, proves that there is no such thing as Native American literature—at least, no such thing as Native American novels anyway. If Silko is right, that the particular language being used is of less importance than "words from the heart," then novels, and Native American novels in particular, are nothing more than fluff.[2] It would be easier and much faster to stick to didactic speeches. If Silko is right, then one would expect to see ethnographies on the best-seller lists instead of her novels. But Silko is wrong, and, like it or not, her words (and those of every other Native American writer), and how she uses them, are why she is read at all. Only by *not* looking at the words, only by *not* interrogating language could anyone claim that myth and language and culture are constituent elements of Native

American fiction. They are not. They are stage props. They are on the stage but they are not the play.

What then, are myth and Native American languages doing in Native American fiction? Myth and Native American language in fiction are not conveyors of cultural sensibilities or cultural truths. But they do have a function and a legacy in the literature. They embody (if myths have bodies), they inscribe the longing for culture, much as a dream catcher, three hubcaps, and reservation plates embody our idea of an "Indian car." The presence of myth and language suggests an intense emotional longing for culture, but they are not culture. This intense longing (think of Tayo in *Ceremony* or Lipsha in *Love Medicine* or Little Tree) is used to transcend barriers of language, of culture, to make lasting what is otherwise periodized by oral performance and ceremonial enactment.

Native American literature, if there is such a thing, does not constitute culture. It constitutes *desire* with seemingly culturally derived forms. To return to the opening statement of this essay, it is LITERATURE that creates the fantasy of the "NATIVE AMERICAN"—not the other way around.

By providing narratives that use desire—desire calling on cultural forms pulled from the contexts and languages that give them meaning—to bridge the gaps between feelings of connection and displacement, we (writers) have created narratives that bleed out our rich cultural specificities into the world, translated and trammeled. How can anything be a translation if the original ground and primary languages are forgotten?

THE NON-EXISTENCE OF NATIVE AMERICAN FICTION

By declaring that what we write is Indian literature—because of the mere presence of myth, of Native
American words, or the origin of the author—without
first looking closely at language and its use, without
looking at art and artistry, we seek to transcend our
heritages instead of continuing them and we kill the
literature in the process. The answer to the question
of what makes these stories Indian stories is much
the same as what turns the Chevy I mentioned a moment ago into an Indian car—the force of our desire
for it to be so. Yet when the Chevy is sold—and here
lies the root of the problem—it ceases to be an Indian
car. It is just a bad car with bald tires. So, too, with
our literature—when we seek to define our genre out
of an emotional urge, without taking pleasure in our
cultural specificities (language, socially constituted
myth, and locally enacted customs) for their own sake,
our literature will always be secondary to its concerns:
as if the illusion has created the illusionist, not the
other way around.

If we aren't careful about how we use, and how we
interpret, literary devices and cultural forms we run
terrible and painful risks of misusing and misunderstanding both. With Native American cultures and
Native languages imperiled, it is especially important
to consider language and its use.

Many of the writers discussed in the preceding
essays are in the ironic position of trying to arrive
at difference through the familiar. What is the point,
after all, of promoting literature in English as the
repository of the remnants of oral tradition, mythic

tropes, and "ways of being," and then getting angry when "non-Indians" such as Forrest Carter utilize the same modes? If the most highly valued words in Indian life and literature are those spoken from the heart, why isn't anyone in a rush to claim *The Education of Little Tree* for the people? We commit ourselves to the task of having to police the boundaries of our domain by enacting pale versions of our culture on the page while relying on a discourse of blood to protect our cultural resources. This is little more than the literary equivalent of a badge and gun: a symbol of our pledge to protect and serve, and the means to do so.

Our written literature in English is responsive to a set of historical circumstances, inventive in its evasiveness, rich in its suggestive capabilities, but ultimately, it is not culture. Books are not reality, and prose, in English, is not a culture, and should not be put in the position of trying to duplicate it. It seems that readers and writers of Native American literature have made the mistake of assuming that writing and culture are interchangeable. One can write from a culture. One can suggest myth. One can craft prose to sound "speakerly," but it cannot speak. (Can the subaltern speak? Yes. But only in a whisper.) We can evoke a connection to the past in our writing, but novels are wishes, fantasies, fairy tales. Writing doesn't represent reality; it creates new realities. Literature has reality, but not life, to offer. And if we insist on asking our writers and demanding of our prose to give us stories that represent instead of

THE NON-EXISTENCE OF NATIVE AMERICAN FICTION

create, we ignore the gifts our cultures and languages have left us and limit ourselves in what our art can potentially offer.

What I love about my cultural patrimony is the life it provides, not the material. What is priceless about my language is not what it means to speak Ojibwe, but what Ojibwe, in its beautiful, tricky turns, means. What is beautiful about good prose, language, and experience itself, is specificity—there is more richness in detail than in any generalization, and the use of Native American languages and mythic types in literature, so far, has ignored the trove of beauty that is our lived linguistic heritage for the gushing well of communicability. Perhaps we have been so misunderstood for so long, we don't know how to stop answering the world, in the broadest possible terms, and this, to me, is a tragedy.

Our experiences and positions as Native Americans inflect our work but shouldn't determine it—the quality of our writing should; the layering of detail, the building of unseen worlds, the uses of our languages as conveyors of beauty and meaning in their own right. Instead of making language jump across the chasm of culture, we should make our readers jump over the canyon of difference. We should be free to construct narratives unchained from the projects of historicizing and pointing away, always away, from our cultural centers, and instead, claim the rights that other writers have enjoyed for centuries: to make larger the worlds of our prose through significant linguistic and cultural detail.

If, instead of seeing literature and language this way, we mix our realities with our fictions so much that our imagined voices become confused with our lived ones, we risk making Statius's mistake of bowing down before Virgil—"forgetting we are empty semblances and taking shadows for substances."[3] Or, perhaps more culturally appropriate, we make the mistake of the common loon (incidentally the chieftain clan among the Ojibwe) who answers his own call echoed back from the next lake over, and, unaware of the mistake, he is urged to call again, and again—only to remain eternally thwarted.

THE NON-EXISTENCE OF NATIVE AMERICAN FICTION

Endnotes

Introduction: The Clouds Overhead

1. R. P. Blackmur, *Language as Gesture* (New York: Columbia University Press, 1980), 378.

2. Charles Baudelaire, *Selected Writings on Art and Literature* (New York: Penguin USA, 1992), 333. In the present translation the translator uses the word "exchange" instead of "transform"—the substitution is mine, in closer keeping to the original intent of the article. Thanks to John Logan for parsing this for me.

3. George Bird Grinnell, *The Fighting Cheyennes* (Williamstown: Corner House Publishers, 1976), 137–138.

4. From the introduction by Hugh Holman. William Gilmore Simms, *The Yemassee,* edited and with an introduction by Hugh Holman (Boston: Houghton Mifflin, 1961), xviii. Also see Hugh Holman's book *The Roots of Southern Writing: Essays on the Literature of the American South* (Athens: University of Georgia Press, 1972).

5. Ibid., xi.

6. Ibid.

7. Ibid., 4.

8. Ibid., 5.

9. Nathaniel Hawthorne, *The House of the Seven Gables* (New York: Penguin Books, 1989), 1–2.

10. Simms, *The Yemassee,* 6.

11. Ibid., xv.

12. John Nichols, "Chant to the Fire-fly: A Philological Problem in Ojibwe." *Journal of Algonquian and Iroquian Linguistics,* Memoir #8 (1991), 116. All quotes from Schoolcraft, Hymes, and

the double-vowel rendition of the Chant are taken from John Nichols's excellent article. Special thanks to John Nichols for proofing and weighing in on the Ojibwe text and my parsing of it.

13. Arnold Krupat, "On the Translation of Native American Song and Story: A Theorized History," in *On the Translation of Native American Literatures,* Brian Swann, editor (Washington, D.C.: Smithsonian Institution Press, 1992), 7.

14. Nichols, "Chant to the Fire-fly," 113.

15. Krupat, "On the Translation of Native American Song and Story," 7.

16. Ibid., 25.

17. Alexander Pope, *Essay on Man and Other Poems* (New York: Dover Publications, 1994), 48.

18. Sherman Alexie, "Every Little Hurricane," in *The Lone Ranger and Tonto Fistfight in Heaven* (New York: Harper-Collins, 1994), 5.

19. Hawthorne, 2–3.

Smartberries

1. Louise Erdrich, *Love Medicine* (New York: Harper-Perennial, 1993), 1.

2. Ibid., 4.

3. Ibid., 7.

4. Hertha D. Sweet Wong, ed., *Louise Erdrich's* Love Medicine: *A Casebook* (New York: Oxford University Press, 2000), 88.

5. Ibid.

6. Paula Gunn Allen, *The Sacred Hoop: Recovering the Feminine in American Indian Traditions* (Boston: Beacon Press, 1992), 240–241.

7. Ibid., 241.

8. Eric Auerbach, *Mimesis: The Representation of Reality in Western Literature,* trans. Willard R. Trask (Princeton: Princeton University Press, 1953), 3–34.

9. Allan Chavkin, *The Chippewa Landscape of Louise Erdrich's* Love Medicine (Tuscaloosa: University of Alabama Press), 2.

10. Ibid., 86.

11. Erdrich, 19.

12. Ibid., 34.

13. Ibid., 12.

14. Ibid., 14.

15. Ibid., 15.

16. Ibid., 41.

17. Ibid., 42.

18. Ibid., 43.

19. Ibid., 1.

20. James Ruppert, "Celebrating Culture," in Hertha D. Sweet Wong, ed., *Louise Erdrich's* Love Medicine: *A Casebook*, 71.

21. Ibid.

22. Stéphane Mallarmé, *Oeuvres complètes*, eds. Henri Mondor and G. Jean-Aubry, trans. Albert Sonnenfeld, Bibliothèque de la Pléiade (Paris: Gallimard, 1945), 869.

23. Rose Foss, "Why Wenabozho Is So Smart," in *Oshkaabewis Native Journal*, 4:1 (1997): 33–34. Transcribed by Giles Delisle and re-transcribed in the double-vowel orthography by Anton Treuer.

24. Collins Oakgrove, "Wenabozho and the Smartberries" in *Living Our Language: Ojibwe Tales and Oral Histories*, ed. Anton Treuer (St. Paul: Minnesota Historical Society Press, 2001), 172.

25. Erdrich, 32.

26. Louise Erdrich, *The Antelope Wife* (New York: Harper-Collins, 1998), 133–134.

27. Ibid., 135.

28. Ibid., 104.

29. Erdrich, *Love Medicine*, 101–102.

30. Ibid., 103.

31. Ibid.

Lonely Wolf

1. Forrest Carter, *The Education of Little Tree* (Albuquerque: University of New Mexico Press, 1989), 4.

2. Leslie Marmon Silko, *Yellow Woman and a Beauty of*

Spirit: Essays on Native American Life Today (New York: Simon and Schuster, 1996), 48–50.

Plain Binoculars

1. These comments are drawn from a number of sources. Dee Brown said "the closest we will ever come in literature to an understanding of what life was like for a western Indian" in his review of *Fools Crow* in the *Chicago Sun-Times,* but it was taken from the jacket of the book. The comment about the "conceptual horizon" comes from: Louis Owens, *Other Destinies: Understanding the American Indian Novel* (Norman: University of Oklahoma Press, 1992), 157. And "finding a lifestyle preserved for a century and reanimated for our benefit and education" is what a reviewer in *Library Journal* had to say, but it is taken from the Amazon.com web site.

2. James Welch, *Fools Crow* (New York: Penguin Books, 1986), 3.

3. Ibid., 6.

4. Ibid., 5.

5. Ibid., 49.

6. Ibid.

7. Ibid., 56–57.

8. Ibid., 117–118.

9. Ibid., 294–295.

10. Ibid., 163.

11. Ibid., 261.

12. Ibid., 42.

13. Ibid., 351–352.

14. Homer, *The Odyssey,* trans. Robert Fagles (New York: Penguin Books, 1996), 157–158.

15. Eric Auerbach, *Mimesis: The Representation of Reality in Western Literature,* trans. Willard R. Trask (Princeton: Princeton University Press, 1953), 3–34.

16. Homer, *The Odyssey,* 14–18. This note and the quotes from Parry are taken from Bernard Knox's brilliant introduction to *The Odyssey.*

17. George Bird Grinnell, *Blackfeet Indian Stories* (Helena: Riverbend Publishing, 2005), 29.

18. Margaret Mead and Ruth Bunzel, eds., *The Golden Age of*

NATIVE AMERICAN FICTION: A USER'S MANUAL

American Anthropology (New York: George Braziller, 1960), 114. Found in Cynthia Parson, *George Bird Grinnell: A Biographical Sketch* (New York: University Press of America, 1992), 7.

19. Seamus Heaney, *Beowulf* (New York: Farrar, Straus, and Giroux, 2000), xxvii.

20. James Fenimore Cooper, *The Last of the Mohicans* (New York: Penguin Classics, 1986), 239.

21. Welch, *Fools Crow*, 8.

22. Ibid., 353–354.

23. Ibid., 355.

24. Ibid., 356.

25. Thomas Mann, *The Magic Mountain*, trans. John E. Woods (New York: Vintage, 1996), xi.

The Myth of Myth

1. Leslie Marmon Silko, *Ceremony* (New York: Penguin Books, 1986), 7.

2. Ibid., 53.

3. Ibid., 5–6.

4. Ibid., 14.

5. Ibid., 36–37.

6. Ibid., 125.

7. Ibid., 125–126.

8. Ibid., 168.

9. Ibid., 177.

10. Ibid., 177–178.

11. Ibid., 180–181.

12. Ibid., 215, 217–218.

13. Ibid., 219.

14. Ibid., 231–232.

15. Ibid., 232.

16. Ibid., 246.

17. Ibid., 253.

18. Ibid., 5–6.

19. François-René de Chateaubriand, *Atala/René* (Berkeley: University of California Press, 1980), 45–46.

20. Silko, 48–49.

21. Ibid., 256.

22. Ibid.

23. Ibid., 168.

24. Ibid., 124.

25. Ibid., 180–181.

26. Ernest Hemingway, "Fathers and Sons" in *The Short Stories* (New York: Scribner's, 1986), 497.

27. Silko, 152.

28. Ibid., 158.

29. Ibid., 252.

30. *The Holy Bible,* containing the Old and New Testaments (Dallas: The Melton Book Company, 1952), 759.

31. John Milton, *Areopagitica* (taken from Renascence Editions: http//: darkwiwng.uoregon.edu/~rbear/arepagitica.html), 12.

32. Leslie Marmon Silko, *Yellow Woman and a Beauty of Spirit: Essays on Native American Life Today* (New York: Simon and Schuster, 1996), 48–50.

33. Ibid., 50.

34. Silko, *Ceremony,* 1.

35. John Hollander, *Rhyme's Reason: A Guide to English Verse* (New Haven: Yale University Press, 1989), 1.

36. Ibid.

37. Milton, 3.

38. Marcel Proust, preface to *Jean Santeuil* (New York: Penguin Books, 1985), xvi.

39. Charles Baxter, *Burning Down the House* (St. Paul: Graywolf Press, 2001).

40. Hemingway, 498.

Indian/Not-Indian Literature

1. Joseph Bruchac, review of *The Education of Little Tree, Parabola.*

2. Rennard Strickland, foreword to Forrest Carter, *The Education of Little Tree* (Albuquerque: University of New Mexico Press, 1989), vi.

3. Sherman Alexie, *Indian Killer* (New York: Warner Books, 1996), 58–59.

4. Ibid., 66.

5. Sherman Alexie, *Reservation Blues* (New York: Atlantic Monthly Press, 1995), 306.

6. Ibid., 10.

7. Ibid.

8. Ibid., 284.

9. Ibid., 17.

10. Ibid., 96–97.

11. Carter, *The Education of Little Tree,* 8.

12. Alexie, *Reservation Blues,* 4.

13. Ibid., 10.

14. Ibid., 13.

15. Ibid., 9.

16. Ibid., 57.

17. Ibid., 11.

18. Carter, 35.

19. Aristotle, *The Complete Works: The Revised Oxford Translation* (Princeton: Princeton University Press, 1991), 2319.

20. Carter, 3.

21. Ibid., 4.

22. Ibid., 5.

23. Ibid.

24. Ibid., 8.

25. Ibid., 123.

26. James Fenimore Cooper, *The Last of the Mohicans* (New York: Penguin Books, 1986), 63.

27. Alexie, *Reservation Blues,* 283.

28. Ibid., 3.

29. Ibid., 7.

30. Ibid., 8–9.

31. Matthew Fleischer, "Navahoax," *LA Weekly,* 23 January 2006.

32. Ted Conover, "A Soul That Won't Heal," *The New York Times,* 15 October 2000.

33. The quotes from the *Minneapolis Star Tribune* and *Esquire* appear on the jacket copy of Nasdijj's book. Many thanks to Tara Smith for her work and ideas on Nasdijj.

34. Fleischer, *op. cit.*

35. Italo Calvino, *Six Memos for the Next Millennium* (Cambridge: Harvard University Press, 1988), 31.

36. Ibid., 32.

ENDNOTES

Some Final Thoughts about the Non-Existence
of Native American Fiction

1. Cleanth Brooks and Robert Penn Warren, *Understanding Poetry: An Anthology for College Students* (New York: Henry Holt, 1938), iv.

2. Leslie Marmon Silko, *Yellow Woman and the Beauty of Spirit: Essays on Native American Life Today* (New York: Simon & Schuster, 1996).

3. Dante Alighieri, *Purgatorio* (New York: Penguin Books, 1995).

DAVID TREUER is Ojibwe from the Leech Lake Reservation in northern Minnesota. He is the author of three novels, *The Translation of Dr Apelles, The Hiawatha,* and *Little.* He teaches literature and creative writing at the University of Minnesota and divides his time between Minneapolis and Leech Lake.

Native American Fiction: A User's Manual has been typeset in Minion Pro, a typeface designed by Robert Slimbach and issued by Adobe in 1989. Book design by Wendy Holdman. Composition at Prism Publishing Center. Manufactured by Edwards Brothers on acid-free paper.